NEWFOUNDLAND

10TH PROVINCE OF CANADA

JOHN PARKER, M.P.

NEWFOUNDLAND
10th PROVINCE OF CANADA

LINCOLNS-PRAGER (PUBLISHERS), LTD.
LONDON.

LINCOLNS-PRAGER (PUBLISHERS), LTD.
3 KENTON STREET,
LONDON, W.C.I.
1950

LETTERPRESS PRINTED IN GREAT BRITAIN
BY SURREY FINE ART PRESS, LTD., REDHILL, SURREY.

CONTENTS

		Page
PREFACE		7
1. LAND AND PEOPLE		9
2. POLITICAL AND ECONOMIC DEVELOPMENT (1728-1934) ...		20
3. COMMISSION GOVERNMENT (1934-1949)		27
4. MACHINERY OF GOVERNMENT		35
5. FISHERIES		49
6. TIMBER PRODUCTS		59
7. MINERALS AND WATER POWER		68
8. MERCHANDIZING AND SECONDARY INDUSTRIES		74
9. TRANSPORT AND COMMUNICATIONS		80
10. AGRICULTURE		92
11. CO-OPERATIVE AND TRADE UNION MOVEMENTS ...		105
12. TOURISM		111
13. EDUCATION AND HOUSING		120
14. HEALTH AND OTHER SOCIAL SERVICES		132
15. THE LABRADOR		139
16. CONFEDERATION AND AFTER		144
APPENDIX 1 BIBLIOGRAPHY		149
APPENDIX 2 NEWFOUNDLAND POPULATION—RECENT CHANGES		151
INDEX		153

ILLUSTRATIONS AND MAPS

CARMANVILLE—CHURCH ... ... *Facing page* 16

HARBOUR BRETON ... ... ,, ,, 17

COUNTRYSIDE ON WEST COAST ... ... ,, ,, 32

SCENERY ON EAST COAST ... ... ,, ,, 33

ST. JOHN'S HARBOUR ... ... ,, ,, 48

SPLITTING CODFISH ... ... ,, ,, 48

POUCH COVE—LANDING STAGE ... ... ,, ,, 49

CORNER BROOK—PAPER MILL ... ... ,, ,, 64

GRAND FALLS ... ... ,, ,, 65
    VIEW OF TOWN (C.1919)
    A PART OF TOWN TODAY

FIRST PLANE TO CROSS ATLANTIC ... ... ,, ,, 80

CODROY VALLEY ... ... ,, ,, 81

MAP OF CORMACK LAND SETTLEMENT ... ... *page* 95

ROBINSONS—GOVERNMENT BULLDOZERS ... ... *Facing page* 96

ST. JOHN'S—SOME NEW HOUSES ... ... ,, ,, 96

HEATHERTON—FARMERS BUILD WINTER STOREHOUSE ,, ,, 96

A FISHING PARTY ... ... ,, ,, 97

LOMOND (BONNE BAY)—VIEW ... ... ,, ,, 112

GRAND FALLS—HIGH SCHOOL ... ... ,, ,, 112

ST. JOHN'S—VIEW ... ... ,, ,, 113

POUCH COVE—FISHING ROOMS ... ... ,, ,, 128

LOMOND (BONNE BAY)—MODERN FISH PLANT ... ,, ,, 128

ST. JOHN'S—SHIPS ... ... ,, ,, 129

PREFACE

BETWEEN July, 1945, and May, 1946, I occupied the post of Parliamentary Secretary for the Dominions and had the departmental responsibility of looking after the affairs of Newfoundland which then came under the supervision of the British Dominions Office. I found the problems of this island fascinating as discussions were then in progress as to its political and economic future. On leaving office I maintained the interest then acquired and decided to write this book as some contribution towards making Newfoundland's problems better known and appreciated on both sides of the Atlantic. I had the good fortune to spend the early autumn of 1948 in the island following up questions in which I had become interested and seeing for myself both the country and many of the personalities concerned.

I should like in particular to thank Sir Gordon MacDonald (now Lord MacDonald), who was then the Governor of Newfoundland, both for helping me to see so much of the country during my visit and for reading and criticizing the first draft of this book. I also should like to thank Mr. P. D. H. Dunn, one of the former Commissioners, for his valuable criticisms.

During my visit to Newfoundland I received a warm welcome and courteous assistance from the many Newfoundlanders with whom I came in contact, whether they were fishermen, loggers and railway workers or teachers or clergy. I should specially like to thank the Commissioners and leading civil servants who gave me so much information about their work, representatives of the paper companies who showed me not only their mills but took me into the wilds to see their logging and road construction, Mr. Gushue of the Fisheries Board and many business men. Magistrate Scott, of the St. Georges District, gave me an insight into the development of the south-west of the island and of the positive help which farmer and fisherman could receive from government. Squadron Leader Pattison was my host during my stays at Gander, which were partly intended and partly a result of the weather. Mr. Ned Christian proved an admirable companion, driving my rail taxi through stretches of jungle-like forest and open barrens where there were no roads. Thanks to his skill we always made the next siding before a freight train came the other way. I should also like to thank the many wives who made me welcome in their homes, often at very short notice. The Grenfell Association and Moravian Mission both helped me by giving full accounts of their activities.

I should like to make it quite clear that all the views expressed in this book are my own and that I take full responsibility for them. I hope that the book may be some contribution towards helping the people of Newfoundland in the big job that lies ahead of them following the important political decisions which they have recently taken.

In conclusion I should like to thank my secretary, Mrs. Pettigrew, for coming along to the House of Commons at all sorts of hours to take down my dictation in the intervals between Divisions. Last but not least my wife has read through the typescript and suggested many valuable improvements.

September, 1949.

JOHN PARKER,
HOUSE OF COMMONS,
WESTMINSTER.

I

LAND AND PEOPLE

STRETCHING far out into the Atlantic, Newfoundland is that part of North America nearest to Europe. Always of great strategic significance, the development of air transport has made it vitally important both in war and peace for those wishing to control the North Atlantic approaches to North America and its contacts with Europe.

Newfoundland lies across the Gulf of St. Lawrence near its northern outlet; it is an island somewhat larger than Ireland in size and has a population of over 325,000.

Despite its comparatively southern latitude its climate is certainly not comparable with France and countries of a similar situation in Europe. A cold Arctic current comes down the Labrador coast to meet, off Newfoundland, a warm flow of water coming up the American coast from Florida. The resulting conflict of temperatures and waters produces a cool variable climate and creates, along the coasts and neighbouring banks, inexhaustible fishing grounds which are the richest in the world. The fogs, for which the country is renowned are, in fact, not widespread far from the south-east coast. Icebergs coming down from the north frequently invade the east coast harbours as late as June and delay the advent of summer. The autumn, however, in all parts of the island, is prolonged and one of the pleasantest times of the year. The west coast of Newfoundland, which faces Canada across the Gulf of St. Lawrence, has a more continental climate, being not only colder in winter but far hotter in the summer.

Most of the island is wild and uninhabited. It consists of barren rocks, lakes, moors and bogs and extensive areas, where the soil is of greater depth and better drained, which are covered with dense and mainly coniferous forests. There are no great heights although the Long Range, well over 1,000 feet in height, runs down the west coast and there are hilly " barrens " in many other parts of the island. The Lewis Hills (2,673 feet),

Gros Morne (2,651 feet) and other points in the west exceed 2,000 feet. The fairly heavy rainfall fills the innumerable rivers which drain the lakes and marshes. The Humber on the west coast and the Exploits and Gander on the north are the most important of these. The forests not only provide fuel and building material but the raw material for the important paper industry. The lakes and rivers provide power as well as salmon and trout for the native and visiting tourist. The sea and its bays provide a livelihood for the island's large fishing population.

One of the largest iron deposits in the world is being mined at Bell Isle; there are also large scale mining operations at Buchans in the centre of the island which produce zinc and other minerals. Fluorspar is obtained in substantial quantities at St. Lawrence on the south coast of the Burin Peninsula. Other minerals are not found at present in easily workable quantities.

The population, which is chiefly engaged in the fisheries, is largely scattered around the very indented coastline in a vast number of small settlements known as " outports." Practically the only settlements away from the coast are along the railways and are connected with the paper industry, civil aviation or mining. Most of the small patches of more fertile soil lie along the warmer west coast. So far, however, there has been comparatively little agricultural development save around St. John's and more recently on the west coast. Much of the population's foodstuffs is still imported even when it could be produced locally.

North of Newfoundland lies the very extensive dependency of Labrador which is about 120,000 square miles in area with a population of under 6,000. Its value to Newfoundland is potential rather than actual. Along its coastline Newfoundlanders carry on summer fisheries. In its interior enormous deposits of iron ore have been found adjoining the Quebec boundary. Hamilton Falls provides one of the largest untapped resources of hydro-electric power in the world. The vast forests of the Hamilton River valley and of southern Labrador have hardly yet been touched. For some time Newfoundland has hoped that development of Labrador would be a source of increased wealth and an outlet for her increasing population. Union with Canada should hasten such development.

At the time of its discovery by Cabot, Newfoundland was inhabited by an American Indian tribe, the Boethics; Eskimos visited its north coast for hunting in the winter. During the 18th century the Micmacs, another Indian tribe, invaded the island from Nova Scotia. Reduced in numbers by their continuous wars with the Micmacs, the Boethics, who retired to the neighbourhood of Red Indian Lake in the middle of the island, were wiped out by the English early in the 19th century. A Micmac village survives at the head of one of the inlets on the south coast and there are two settlements of Jackatars on the west coast; these are a mixture of French and Indians. Unlike the Micmacs the Jackatars have a reputation for immorality and thieving.

About two-thirds of Newfoundland's present European population came from the English West Country, mainly from Somerset, Dorset and Devon. Over a fourth probably came from Ireland[1] and a substantial number from the Channel Islands[2]. Early settlers on the west coast included some French Acadians and Scottish Highlanders who came over from Nova Scotia; they were joined by a small number of fishermen from France who deserted their vessels during the 19th century to escape conscription. A sprinkling of Syrians and Jews entered in the early 20th century to establish shops and small businesses especially in the new paper towns. A few Scandinavians came to take part in the fisheries.

Before the discovery of America, fishermen of England, France, Spain and Portugal were already going as far afield as Iceland. Within a few years of this discovery they were crossing the Atlantic to exploit Newfoundland's codfish. Coming over each year in their small boats with favourable easterly winds in the spring they returned heavily laden each autumn with their dry salted cod assisted by winds which, at that time of year, were mainly westerly. The numerous bays and harbours of the island were filled with ships of a wide variety of nationalities who landed and set up their " stages " for drying their fish. First arrivals each year were recognized as occupiers of a particular site for that season. The English

---

[1] In the 1945 census the number of people who stated that they were of Irish " ethnic origin " was so substantially less than those of Roman Catholic faith that many of mixed English and Irish extraction must have recorded themselves as of English " ethnic origin."

[2] Surprisingly there is no separate entry in the census records for those of Channel Islands " ethnic origin."

and French gradually became the dominant elements among the European visitors, the French being in the main drawn from Brittany, Normandy, Poitou and the Basque country. Sir Humphrey Gilbert took possession of Newfoundland officially of behalf of England in 1583 but did not establish any enduring settlement. Early in the next century a number of parties began to stay behind throughout the winter in order to be able to retain control of fishing stages from year to year and to look after property that had been left behind. The first English settlements were in Conception Bay (Cupids—1610) and in Ferryland (Trepassey—1615). At an early date St. John's became their principal headquarters owing to its excellent harbour. The French were not to be outdone and established Placentia on the opposite side of the Avalon Peninsula (1662) and fortified it both as a centre to safeguard their fisheries and also to control the route up the St. Lawrence to their colony of Canada. After a good deal of fighting Placentia was finally taken by the English and its inhabitants expelled; the Treaty of Utrecht (1713) confirmed Britain in the ownership of Newfoundland.

Further attacks, however, took place upon the English settlements until the final cession of Canada to Britain (1763). This guaranteed the French various fishing rights along the coast of Newfoundland and gave them the small islands of St. Pierre and Miquelon off its south coast as a headquarters for their fishing fleet. This treaty marked the beginning of a long conflict with the French over their fishing rights which did not terminate until the Anglo-French Treaty of 1904.

Despite the quarrel with France, the English West Country fishery interests were not keen to encourage settlements in Newfoundland. The trade had come to be dominated largely by big merchants in Poole and Bristol who financed the fitting out of the vessels for their yearly visits. They feared that any large scale settlement in the island would lead to a gradual transfer of this remunerative trade to the settlers. The Admiralty backed them up as it regarded the fisheries as an admirable training ground for British seamen. Despite all their efforts, however, small numbers of fishermen continued to stay behind and gradually brought over their families to join them. Many attempts were made to prevent them from cultivating the soil and thus trying to provide part of their foodstuffs   Right through the 17th and 18th centuries the number of settlers remained small and there was a steady drift from among them to New England. Newfoundland was regarded more as a " great ship moored near the fishing banks " than as a colony.

The Seven Years' War and the American War of Independence both increased the number of settlers owing to the wartime dangers in crossing the Atlantic. It was the French Revolutionary and Napoleonic wars, however, which completely altered the situation. The attacks of French privateers on the fishing fleets at sea and fear of the press gang at home led a steady stream of settlers to establish themselves despite all the protests of West Country merchants and of the British Government. As late as 1792, 276 vessels from the West Country, mainly bankers, crossed the Atlantic to take part in the fisheries; in 1817 these numbers had shrunk to 48 and six years later to 15. In 1783 the winter population of Newfoundland was about 10,000 but by 1815 it was approximately 40,000; most of this increase had taken place after 1800.

At the beginning of these wars the total catch of fishing boats fitted out in England still greatly exceeded that of the boats belonging to the settlers. By the end of the wars this position had been completely reversed.

The steady flow of migrants across the Atlantic continued during the twenties and thirties although the rate declined as the number of English vessels making yearly crossings became less and less and finally stopped altogether. From then onwards Newfoundland's steady growth of population has been primarily due to natural increase which carried it to 146,536 (1869), 197,859 (1884), 221,000 (1901) and 321,000 (1945), when 98.5 per cent was Newfoundland born. This large increase has taken place despite a steady migration from the middle of the 19th century onwards to Canada and U.S.A. The French fishermen have continued until the present day to cross the Atlantic yearly to make use of their fishing base in the islands of St. Pierre and Miquelon, which were restored to France in 1815. Their winter population of 4,200 is raised to over 10,000 in summer.

From their earliest settlements in the Avalon Peninsula settlers had spread up the north-east coast as far as Twillingate by 1700 and along the south coast later in the 18th century. In their schooners they pushed to the head of bays and inlets to establish their winter settlements. Many a fisherman planted his home just within sight of the home of his nearest neighbour. It was not until they had covered the greater part of the coastline in this manner that they gradually began to come together into villages or " outports." In many cases these were largely inhabited by members of the same family who remained living in adjacent houses when the original settler's children grew up.

The first area of close settlement was in the Avalon Peninsula especially around Conception Bay, whose outports, some of which were comparatively populous, took an active part in the seal, Labrador and other fisheries. Harbour Grace was long the second town in the island and its population reached 7,054 in 1884. A decline then started in the population of the whole of this area which has continued to the present day as the people have moved to other parts of the island or gone overseas. The last census (1945) gave the town of Harbour Grace a population of only 2,065. The population of the barren south coast, which is also remote from the logging areas, has remained static in recent years despite an important local development of quick freezing fish plants.

The treaty rights of the French and Americans delayed settlement of the warmer and more fertile west coast. Despite the strong opposition of the British Government, in addition to that of the French and Americans, settlers gradually moved in to the principal western bays and inlets as well as on to the coast of the long northern peninsula known as Petty Nord. A small settlement had been made at the end of the 18th century in Bay St. Georges. By 1881 there were some 9,000 settlers on the west coast who had increased to over 17,000 by 1901. Recent census figures[1] show a continuance of the pronounced drift of people to the west and north-east coasts and to the paper towns in particular. The capital has also grown rapidly as have the mining communities, especially Bell Island.

In early years many of the settlers lived on the coast in summer and moved up the rivers or to the heads of bays in the winter to more sheltered spots where fuel was more easily come by. This custom, which still continues in parts of Labrador, disappeared in most parts of Newfoundland in the early 19th century as settlers began to cultivate the garden plots around

[1] See Appendix 2.

their houses and keep a few cows and chicken; they finished their fishing in the autumn sufficiently early not only to enable them to dig their potatoes but also to cut sufficient wood for the winter and, if necessary, either bring it in by water or by dog-sledge.

A few isolated English settlers had been established on the Atlantic coast of Labrador in the 18th century. At that time Eskimos hunted over the whole area as far south as the Gulf of St. Lawrence. They were gradually exterminated, however, in the whole area south of Hamilton Inlet by Indian tribes who found it easier to purchase firearms. Early in the 19th century fishermen from the east and north-east coasts of Newfoundland began to fish during the summer off the Labrador coast. Over 3,000 " Liviers " are now in residence along this coast between Hamilton Inlet and Blanc Sablon at the Quebec border. Most of these came from Newfoundland although a number of Channel Islanders settled directly along the north shore of the straits of Belle Isle. The greater part of the fishing " off the Labrador " is still carried on, however, by fishermen from Newfoundland who prefer to come there only for the summer in the same way as their forefathers came yearly to Newfoundland from the English West Country.

Nearly 1,000 Eskimos and halfbreeds dwell in a number of settlements established by the Moravians in the part of Labrador which is north of the Hamilton Inlet. Some white trappers, many of Scottish origin, have settled along the shores of the Hamilton Inlet, their most important village being Northwest River. The Canadian air base at Goose has brought a new settlement into being nearby at Happy Valley, whose inhabitants are drawn from all parts of Labrador and Newfoundland. The whole of this enormous area still has a population of under 6,000 including a number of Indians who roam about the interior.

When settlement began to grow rapidly in Newfoundland at the end of the 18th century, the British Government encouraged the building of churches and a number of Anglican clergymen came out to minister to the inhabitants. The Irish population which came in was mainly Catholic and was soon supplied with churches and priests. Of the various Nonconformist bodies the Methodists were by far the most successful and merged with most of the others into the United Church in 1926 when that body was set up in Canada. Today just under a third of the population are Anglican, nearly a third Catholic and rather more than a third belong to the United Church, Salvation Army and other Protestant churches.

The census figures show considerable changes in the relative strength of the different religious bodies between 1857 and 1945. The Anglicans fell slowly and steadily from 35.6 per cent to 31.3 per cent while the Catholics dropped from 45.8 per cent to 32.9 per cent; their percentage of the population, however, has remained stable since 1921. The Methodists steadily grew from 16.3 per cent in 1857 to 28.2 per cent in 1921; the creation of the United Church was followed by a drop to 24.9 per cent in 1945. The Salvation Army grew continuously from 1 per cent in 1891 to 7 per cent in 1945; the last two decades have also seen the building up of the Jehovah Witnesses (2.3 per cent in 1945). It is significant that the increasing strength of Evangelical Protestantism, which the above figures show, has taken place during a period when immigration had practically ceased and when there was a rapid growth of population by natural increase. The remarkable drop in the Catholic percentage seems to be accounted for, at least in part, by particularly heavy migration overseas to U.S.A. and Canada from strongly Catholic areas in the Avalon Peninsula until checked by American immigration restrictions.

The churches have played a very large part in Newfoundland in building up social consciousness, providing community life and constructing schools. To their teaching is largely due the very small amount of law-breaking in a country with a tiny police force. They established a particularly strong position owing to the absence of local government institutions and the impossibility of effective central administration over such a widely scattered population with so few communications. In the vast majority of the outports the inhabitants almost all belong to the same church which thus becomes the focus of local life.

The Anglicans have had a Bishop in Newfoundland since 1839[1]; they are well distributed, being particularly strong on the south coast and among the English and Channel Island settlers on the west. The Roman Catholics have half the population in St. John's, most of the outports in the south

[1] Joint with Bermuda until 1917.

16

Carmanville—Church, as usual, dominates the outport

Photo: *Newfoundland Tourist Development Board.*

Harbour Breton—A typical outport on south coast

of the Avalon Peninsula, a third of the population in Corner Brook and those sections of the west coast population which are French or Highland Scottish in origin. The Micmacs, Labrador Indians and Jackatars also belong to this faith as do the small Syrian community who are practically all of Lebanese origin. The Roman Catholics have an Archbishop and two bishops, their first bishop having been appointed as early as 1784. The United Church is the strongest on the east and north-east coasts. The population of all the important towns and larger settlements is mixed in religion; the Salvationists are particularly strong in such areas. The Moravians have the support of the Eskimos and halfbreeds in northern Labrador.

Some French and Gaelic are spoken on the west coast but seem to be dying out. The Indians and Eskimos have their own languages. English is taught in all the schools and is understood by practically all Newfoundland's inhabitants. Owing to the isolated nature of many of the settlements there is a wide variety of dialects. Around St. John's an Irish brogue is strong; on parts of the west coast an Ontario accent is becoming widespread. Over a large part of the country, however, English West Country accents, especially those with the strong " r " prevail. Those of Somerset and Dorset seem particularly dominant. Some of the present day inhabitants of my home town, Bristol in England (originally Bridgestow), are still fond of adding an " l " to a word ending with a vowel sound; " idea " is frequently thus pronounced by them as " ideal." I found people who lived in a settlement in Newfoundland which is written on the maps as " Gambo " calling it " Gambol." A large number of old West Country songs and dances survive in Newfoundland forms; many original Newfoundland folk songs, especially sea shanties, are also current.

Newfoundland has developed distinctive word usages of its own; "Christian" names continue to be drawn frequently from the Old Testament. It is claimed that there are 1,000 terms of speech which are peculiar to Newfoundland. " Mullygrubs " and " plawmosh," for example, are local words for grumbling and flattery. Most of the very numerous sheets of water in the country, save the very largest, are known as " ponds," a pointed hill is a " tolt," the head of a bay is a " bottom," and a narrow strait between an island and the mainland is a

17

" tickle." More of the sheets of water are in fact known as ponds than the maps would suggest; I found that Lake St. John was mainly spoken of by loggers as " John's Pond."

Newfoundland's place names are rarely borrowed from other countries and have a variety which is attractive not only on account of their quaintness and sound but from the history, occupations and local character which they show. Jersey Harbour, Famish Cove, Empty Basket, Fox Trap, Whale's Gulch and Newfoundland Dog Pond are a representative sample. Sometimes they are intentionally amusing such as Noggin Cove, Pinchgut Point, Lushes Bight, Ha Ha Bay and Horse Chops. Distinctive practices in Newfoundland are to reverse double names as in Harbour Grace and Bay Bulls and to add an " s " to the name of the original founder of a settlement such as Manuels, Tompkins or Robinsons.

Despite this inventiveness in local geographical terms it was felt necessary to set up a Nomenclature Commission in 1902 owing to the island's " paucity of nomenclature." The number of Seal Coves, Indian Bays, Riverheads, etc., was certainly enormous. There was a widespread desire not only to get rid of some of this duplication but to change names which had become unpopular locally (such as Crabbes) or which a new generation had become squeamish about using which included terms such as gut, hole, backside, etc. The Nomenclature Commission which included the Minister of Posts, representative clergy and people with an interest in the country's history, made a number of sweeping changes in its early years which placed names such as Curling, Hampden, Botwood, Windsor, St. David's, Eastport and Lourdes on the map. Saints' names were frequently introduced when renaming Catholic outports. The Board strongly opposed the widespread desire to add the word " ville " as a termination. In recent years it has discouraged any further change of name without very good reason and was, with great difficulty, persuaded to accept " Gander " as the name for Newfoundland's airport. The selection of " Cormack " as a name for the new land settlement on the upper Humber was a happy way of commemorating the man who first crossed Newfoundland from coast to coast.

Italian and Portuguese explorers named places such as Bonavista, Conception Bay and Cape Race on the east coast. Many French names survive, particularly on the west and south

coasts and around White Bay. Where possible Newfoundlanders pronounce these as though they were English words.
Sometimes they have been Anglicized in spelling as well as
pronunciation. The French name, Barachois, was frequently
given to a wide shallow river with a sandy bar across its mouth
which is found in many parts of the country; it is now usually
pronounced and sometimes written Barasway. In too many
cases, however, the official maps still stick to a form which is
not in common usage; all Newfoundlanders talk about " Bay
Despair "[1] but this large inlet on the south coast is still written
on the maps as " Baie d'Espoir."

It seems a pity that official names in such circumstances cannot be brought into line with popular usage both in spelling
and pronunciation. No new departure of principle would be
involved as this has already been widely done in Newfoundland. There are a small number of place names in Newfoundland of Indian origin (such as " Wabana " on Bell Isle and
the " Annieopscotch Mountains "). There are also a large
number of names of Eskimo origin in Labrador particularly in
its northern parts.

[1] Contributors to the " Book of Newfoundland " give this also as Bay
D'Espair and Baie de Espoir.

POLITICAL DEVELOPMENTS (1728-1934)

THE visiting fishermen had early established a primitive form of self-government in each of the bays or inlets in Newfoundland for settling their quarrels; the first arrival was frequently recognized as Captain for the season with powers of arbitration. This machinery did not work well and the English West Country merchants who controlled the fish trade did their best to oppose the extension of any governmental institutions to the settlers whom they desired to exclude from the island. From 1728 onwards British Governors came out each year for the fishing season and returned for the winter. Once they had gone, there was riot and disorder in many of the settlements. Efforts were made to enforce some measure of law and order by the appointment of magistrates. They were not supposed to sit during the long months when the Governor was absent and, even when he was there, the Governor's attempts to get local legal machinery to work smoothly were interrupted by appeals of the West Country merchants to Courts in England to upset local decisions. Finally, between 1789 and 1791, action was taken, which was confirmed by the British Parliament, to establish a local Supreme Court and to make the legal system work more effectively. This big reform, which was carried out in the teeth of the opposition of the West Country merchants, was intended mainly to serve the needs of the visiting fishing fleets. The settlers still had to crowd their cases in with those of the visitors during the period when the Governor was resident.

The complete change in the situation, which took place during the French Revolutionary wars when the larger part of the local fishery passed into the hands of the residents led, in 1817, to the Governor staying right through the year for the first time. The needs of the colony, which had come into existence despite the home country, had at last to be recognized. In 1824 all the old enactments discouraging settlement were repealed and the island was at last officially raised to the status of a colony. Most of the Governors had hitherto been admirals with comparatively short periods of office. Hamilton (1818-1825) and Cochrane (1825-1834) were not only resident throughout the year but held office long enough to build up some kind of administration. Cochrane, in particular, vigorously threw himself into the building of roads and carrying out other public works. All this helped to develop a sense of budding nationhood.

Even before the outbreak of the French Revolutionary wars, St. John's had become a merchandizing centre. Here stores were brought in for the use both of visiting fishermen and settlers and the dried codfish was purchased for export. Instead of being itself mainly a fishing base it had become a distributing centre for all parts of the island. Many of the West Country merchants and some from the West Indies had opened branches here or had sent out sons or relatives to act as their representatives. A number of one-time local fishermen had also set themselves up as merchants in a small way. Soon the interests of the merchants operating in St. John's came into open conflict with those still living in the West Country, although it remained customary for many years for those who had made money in Newfoundland to retire to England in old age.

As the wealthiest and most influential group in Newfoundland, the St. John's Water Street merchants gave a lead in the fight to remove the old restrictions and soon went on to demand Representative Government. In this they were only demanding that traditional practice in other British Colonies should be followed. The first pamplet urging this had been published in 1812; the campaign succeeded twenty years later (1832).

Between 1832 and 1855 considerable friction existed between the Government and the House of Assembly with the result that the latter was suspended for a few years. Demand for Responsible Government grew and was finally conceded. This meant that Newfoundland was henceforth governed by its own Prime Minister and Cabinet responsible to a locally elected House of Assembly and a Legislative Council appointed by the Queen's representative, the Governor, in consultation with the Prime Minister. Elections were normally held every four years; the House of Assembly usually met only a few months yearly. The franchise was gradually widened. Representation was not given to the west coast until 1881; Labrador was still without representation in 1934. At the termination of Responsible Government (1934) the House of Assembly consisted of 27 Members, having been reduced from 40 in 1932. The Legislative Council consisted of 17 Members appointed for life. After the Statute of Westminster (1931) Newfoundland ranked as a Dominion although the Statute was never ratified by the local parliament.

During almost the whole 80 years of Responsible Government both the Government and Parliament were drawn almost exclusively from the merchant class in general and that of St. John's in particular. This was inevitable as for the greater part of the time they were the only moneyed group in the country with any economic power. At the beginning of the period bitter sectarian strife ended in a number of religious riots (1861). These were followed by an understanding between the three main religious groups to share not only Cabinet offices equally between them but also Government patronage. This sharing of political power certainly had a soothing effect on sectarian quarrels. The entrance of religious tests into the whole governmental field, however, was most unfortunate, stimulating the spoils system and making it impossible to build up an effective civil service. Two main political parties, usually called Liberals and Conservatives, struggled with one another for power, there always being a Government and an Opposition. Whatever their names, these parties differed very little from one another in policy being based largely upon rival personalities and groups among the merchant class. The one necessity about every party was that it must be substantially supported in each of the three main religious groups so that a Cabinet could be constituted equally from all three.

A strong and distinctive local national feeling grew up during this period in Newfoundland which is much stronger than that which commonly exists in an English-speaking Province of Canada or in an American State. The long struggle with the French and Americans over fishing rights on the west and north coasts greatly stimulated this growth of national feeling. Indignation was felt also against the home country whose Government was continually pressing the islanders to observe the terms of the treaties which Britain had made with France and the United States. Many attempts were made to settle outstanding difficulties with both nations; when one problem, such as the Bait Issue, appeared solved however it was followed by another such as the Lobster Controversy. This struggle with the French which started in 1763, was only concluded by the Anglo-French Convention of 1904, while the controversy with the Americans, which started with the recognition of American Independence (1783) only terminated with the Hague Award in 1910. The British Government secured the renunciation of the French claims by making concessions in other parts of the world. The fight for full possession of their country was, however, won by Newfoundlanders who had insisted in settling on the west coast despite all the obstacles placed in their way. By 1904 the French, like English West Countrymen before them, were finding it increasingly difficult to claim rights on behalf of fishermen crossing the Atlantic every summer against men resident on the spot. These long drawn-out battles certainly strengthened national consciousness but delayed the settlement of some of the best parts of the island. This stopped the effective development of agriculture and long confined the island's economy almost entirely to the fisheries.

The lands lying up the St. Lawrence had few contacts with the isolated island of Newfoundland, the vast majority of whose population still lived on its east coast. The fact also that a large part of its trading relations were with Europe and the West Indies had a big influence upon the country's reactions to proposals for joining the Canadian Confederation both when it was first brought into being in the late 1860's and again after the Newfoundland financial crisis of 1894. The Newfoundland Government of the day had taken part in a number of discussions leading up to the creation of the Canadian Confederation and finally recommended joining the new Dominion. As discussion in Parliament and the country developed a strong anti-Confederate movement sprang up led by a wealthy merchant called Bennett. He managed to rally the St. John's merchants by raising fear of Canadian commercial competition, stirred up Irish hatred of the Union of 1801 by comparing Newfoundland's proposed confederation with Canada with that between Great Britain and Ireland and terrified the fishermen in most of the outports by saying that new taxes would be imposed on their boats and gear. The Confederates were decisively defeated in the general election of 1869 by a 2-1 majority. In 1895 the Canadian Government of the day was not particularly sympathetic to the financial needs of the sadly chastened Newfoundland. The breakdown of the negotiations left a feeling of considerable bitterness in Newfoundland allied with some rejoicing among the Water Street merchants that they had after all been able to maintain a separate Newfoundland economy despite all their difficulties.

Through all these discussions there was no very obvious advantage which would come to Newfoundland as a result of Confederation unless the Dominion Government was prepared to offer Newfoundland more favourable terms than to other colonies. The possible reduction in the price of foodstuffs in particular and the cost of living generally was only appreciated by a minority of fishermen mainly in the south-west. The fishermen in the latter part of the 19th century were without any leaders of their own to put forward any criticism of the dominant views of St. John's. The great mass of the population was still resident in the Avalon Peninsula and was, therefore, closely under the influence of the capital.

The first important revolt against the Water Street merchants came in 1908 when Coaker began to organize the Fishermen's Protective Union near Bonavista on the east coast. This stirring orator carried on a raging campaign during the next five years which brought 20,000 fishermen into his organization and succeeded in electing nine Members to the House of Assembly. The F.P.U., under Coaker's leadership, built up a whole series of enterprises at Port Union which aimed at processing fish and bulk purchasing materials for the fishermen. After having a good deal of political and economic influence the movement lost its force when Coaker entered the 1914-18 wartime Coalition and subsequent Cabinets. The main significance of this movement was the indication that fishermen away from St. John's could be organized politically to take a line antagonistic to that of the principal Water Street merchants.

The growth of the paper industry and the steady settlement of the west coast had not had any very big political influence before the end of Responsible Government (1934), although these areas of the country viewed the suspension of Responsible Government with a great deal of relief despite the fact that

24

they had suffered less from the very lean years of the slump (1929-1933) than most of the fishing outports.

The Newfoundland Government early realized the undesirability of having all the country's eggs in one basket, namely the fisheries. They, therefore, did their best to encourage development of the copper mines and the construction of the transinsular railroad. The building of the railway was looked upon not only as providing immediate employment but as opening up enormous potential resources. So keen had the country become to get the railway built and operated that the Government gave enormous concessions to the Reid interests which would have handed over control of the island's economy very largely to a particular firm had the agreement remained in operation.

Ruling circles in St. John's came to realize that many services, such as the operation of the railway and coastal steamships, which were vital to the island's economy, could not be carried on remuneratively by private enterprise. The unstable character of the fishing industry and the large amounts of public relief and relief works which had to be financed from time to time had necessitated heavy public expenditure. The Government of the day, therefore, with the general support of public opinion, borrowed extensively in the hope that the expenditure would open up national resources and ultimately add to the national revenue. The construction of the railway certainly enabled the paper mills and Buchans mine to be opened. Much of the Government's expenditure, however, was frittered away and many of the developments this expenditure made possible took a long time to mature. The result was that Newfoundland's Budget did not balance from the 1914-18 war onwards. The depression of 1929-33 hit the island particularly hard and a time came when Newfoundland could no longer borrow and bankruptcy stared the country in the face. Britain was asked to appoint the Amulree Commission to investigate the country's position. When it recommended a suspension of Representative Government and resumption by Britain of responsibility for administering the country its report was accepted by the Government and House of Assembly in default of any other way out of their troubles.

In fairness to the men who governed during the eighty years of Responsible Government, it must be said that they were neither better nor worse than the rulers of many American States or Canadian Provinces during the same period. Some men of outstanding ability such as Bond and Whiteway filled the office of Prime Minister. The comparative poverty of Newfoundland and the instability of its major industry created difficulties which local political leaders were not able to overcome. The evils of the spoils system and the lack of effective administrative machinery became glaring when circumstances forced the Government to take increasing action in the economic field. The ruling merchant class had become unwilling to invest money in enterprises private or public save their own personal businesses. When it became impossible to raise further money from overseas to carry on government they accepted with relief a suspension of Responsible Representative Government which they hoped—and intended—would only be temporary.

3

COMMISSION GOVERNMENT (1934-1949)

THE new Government which was set up as a result of the Amulree Report consisted of an executive Governor and six Commissioners three of whom had to be Newfoundlanders and three British. Both the House of Assembly and Legislative Council were suspended and the Governor and Commission became a legislative as well as an executive body. Proposed changes in the law were first advertised, comments collected upon them and the new laws were then passed at a meeting of the Commission. Extensive changes in the law were thus carried through during the fifteen years of the Commission Government. The House of Assembly had only met for a few months yearly whereas the Commission had weekly meetings for the greater part of the year. Remarkable success attended this law making thanks to the care taken to assess criticism after the first drafts of Bills had been issued to the public.

Newfoundlanders who sat on the Commission were drawn first from the ranks of former political leaders. As a new civil service grew up in the country Commissioners tended to be drawn from its ranks. The British Commissioners were drawn almost entirely from the British—including Indian and Colonial—civil service. Newfoundlanders had the big advantage of continuity, whereas the British suffered from the fact that appointments were made for three years and few were willing to stay away from their home country for more than one period of office. Changes of British personnel were, therefore, far too frequent to make for good government though one or two Commissioners, such as Hope Simpson and Dunn had a very considerable effect upon the Government's policy. Dunn had first served as Customs advisor to the Government and, therefore, knew a good deal about the country before he returned as a Commissioner. It was not realized at first in Whitehall that an executive Governor needed to be a different type of man from the retired naval men who had usually filled the post satisfactorily under Responsible Government. The last

Governor, Macdonald, was the only one appointed specifically on account of his political and administrative experience and social and economic knowledge. Throughout its period of office the Commission Government suffered from the realization that it was intended to be only temporary in character. With all its drawbracks it can claim a remarkably fine record of achievement.

The rule of the Commission Government falls into two periods, the seven years up to 1941 and the eight years following. In the first financial stringency restricted development; in fact some financial help from the British Government was required to make possible what the Government did. During this period the foundation was laid for a modern form of government administration and there was a start to building up social services with the construction of cottage hospitals and new schools. In the economic field the building up of a marketing organization in the fishing industry was begun. Opportunities were taken to start an overhaul of taxation machinery and of tariff policy.

The second period was a very different one. The boom, started by the building of the Canadian and American bases, continued during and after the war. Budget receipts made it possible not only to expand the Government's expenditure enormously but to pile up a large surplus every year. Not only were large scale programs carried through with the building of further new schools and hospitals, but the Government's salaries and services improved all round. An attempt was made to secure the co-operation of private firms in building up a planned economy. Surveys were put in hand to ascertain agricultural, geological, forest and water power resources. Ten-year Reconstruction schemes for development in all important fields were prepared and widely discussed in public. Trade unions, the co-operative movement and local government were all actively encouraged. During this period of remarkable prosperity the standard of life was raised and an effort made to provide Newfoundland with some of the services that had long been lacking.

The Commission Government, however, was far from being generally popular. In its initial stages tactless mistakes had been made, such as the conversion of the House of Assembly into a government office and the closing of a not very adequate museum. Many of the Water Street merchants soon began to regret their loss of political power, especially as the Commission Government was not dominated by the interests of the capital and deliberately encouraged the growth of other social groups in the population. The increase of income tax rates during the war particularly aroused their wrath despite the high profits being made and the fact that the Newfoundland rates of tax still remained behind those of Great Britain and Canada. A vociferous demand for the restoration of self-government arose accompanied by complaints about the wastage on the new social services of money which they would have preferred to have remained in their own pockets. This line was taken despite the fact that the paper and mining industries with their growing prosperity contributed a great deal to the national revenue.

Responsible Government had originally been suspended on the understanding that it would be restored when financial circumstances justified it and when public opinion had expressed such a desire. The abnormal war conditions and the doubt as to whether prosperity would continue when peace returned were held by the British Government to justify the continuance of the Commission at least until the end of the war. A keen division of views in the island as to whether the paper industry and fisheries would continue to be as prosperous once more normal conditions returned, and the doubt as to whether new social services could be built up—or even existing ones maintained—in the future, led the British Government to call a National Convention to discuss the country's future. It was to be asked to formulate alternative issues to place before the country at a referendum for a definite decision.

Arrangements were made to elect, by adult suffrage, 45 members from all parts of the country, including Labrador, to this Convention which met over a period of eighteen months (1946-1948). To prevent the Water Street merchants from unduly dominating the Convention, as they had in the past dominated the House of Assembly, a residence qualification of two years in a constituency for candidates was insisted upon. Only 20 per cent of the electorate troubled to vote. Thirteen of the forty-five who were elected were merchants, most of them being local men buying goods from the St. John's merchants. Three co-operative officials, all from the west coast, and three trade union officers were elected. Others were drawn from a wide variety of occupations though it was significant that no working fisherman was chosen. Delegations were sent by the Convention first to Britain to ascertain whether any more help might be forthcoming and then to Canada to discuss possible terms for Confederation. The long and acrimonious discussions, particularly on the issue of Confederation, did not add to the Convention's prestige. The fact that much of the proceedings was broadcast did, however, have a big influence on public opinion. The Convention's main usefulness was in fact in the field of political education.

Members of the Convention had not been elected on any particular programs as opinion had not crystalized on the main issues which were to come up during its meetings. The Convention ultimately recommended the Government to put the two questions of returning to Responsible Government or a continuation of Commission Government for a further five years before the electors. A proposal also to put Confederation with Canada before the electorate was defeated in the Convention. The Government ultimately decided, however, to put all three issues before the people with the proviso that, if no proposal received an absolute majority, there should be a second referendum to decide between the two proposals which had obtained the largest number of votes.

The two referenda campaigns were fiercely fought during the summer of 1948. A record poll for North America of 85 per cent was obtained. In the first referendum Responsible Government led by a 5,000 majority over Confederation. The proposal to continue the Commission Government for a further five years, however, received a substantial vote despite the fact that members of the Commission had taken no steps to state the case for its continuance. On the second vote most of those who voted for the continuance of the Commission gave their support to Confederation which thus achieved an absolute majority of close on 7,000 votes or about 52 per cent of the votes cast. The following table gives the detailed votes:—

FIRST REFERENDUM

Responsible Government	...	69,400
Confederation	... ...	64,066
Commission ...	... ...	22,311

Confederation	...	...	78,323
Responsible Government	...		71,334

Majority	...	6,989

Opinion ran very high during these campaigns and the Confederate and anti-Confederate parties were well organized. The Confederate victory was an emphatic defeat both for St. John's and for the majority of Water Street merchants. The outports emphatically voted down the capital. Every parliamentary constituency outside the Avalon Peninsula had a Confederate majority whilst every constituency in Avalon had an anti-Confederate majority, St. John's itself was two to one for the anti-Confederates. The vote cut across religious divisions. A large number of Catholics on the Avalon Peninsula opposed Confederation whilst many of their fellow-religionists on the west coast were its enthusiastic supporters.

J. R. Smallwood, a journalist who was the Confederate leader, successfully united the outport fishermen in most parts of the country, the co-operative movement in the west and the majority of the people in the paper industry behind his plea for union with Canada. They felt that they had no chance of obtaining the " baby bonuses " and other social services which Canada was able to provide if Newfoundland remained a small isolated community. There was also a strong belief that, if bad times should ever come again, the common man would have a better chance if he were a member of a larger community. Chesley Crosbie, one of the ablest of the St. John's merchants, put the more moderate case for the immediate restoration of Responsible Government. He tried to counter fears of possible dangers from future isolation by urging the desirability of a commercial agreement with the United States to safeguard the American market for Newfoundland fish. His campaign fell rather flat, however, as he had no such definite proposals to put before the electorate as the preliminary ones that had already been worked out for Confederation with Canada. Crosbie was not helped in his campaign by the violent attacks made on the Commission and all their works and on Confederation by old-time politicians. Active dislike of the kind of government which had been in existence in the days of Responsible Government, and a fear that the Water Street merchants were only waiting for a chance to get their hands on the surplus which had been built up since 1941, played an important part in the final decision. There is little doubt that the big growth of population outside the Avalon Peninsula, although it still had 45 per cent of the total in 1945, combined with the development of new industries and new social and economic forces, took political power away from the large group of Water Street merchants, whose bitter opposition to Confederation was based not only on a desire to keep political power but on their fears of increased economic competition from the other Canadian Provinces.

Opinion in the other Canadian Provinces had been keen to secure Newfoundland as a member of the Confederation in the late 60's when it was first coming into being. Little interest had, however, been shown in 1895 when Newfoundland put forward feelers for joining the Dominion following her own financial crisis of 1894. Despite the lack of enthusiasm in Canada which let this opportunity pass, there was a gradual increase of Canadian contacts during the next sixty years. Firstly, the principal Canadian banks moved in and Newfoundland's currency became linked with that of Canada. Canadian insurance companies also played an increasingly important part in the island. The iron ore mines at Bell Island were constructed and operated by Canadian interests in connection with the steel plant at Cape Breton (Nova Scotia). In recent years Canadian canning companies have begun to enter the island's fish trade. Canadian industrial interests, however, have played a very small part in the island compared with either the British firms dominating the paper trade or the local concerns which control merchandizing and most of the secondary industries.

The Canadian Government, especially after the coming of the Commission Government, increasingly lent officers to Newfoundland to carry out inquiries and assist in starting new services. As educational standards rose a flow of young Newfoundlanders to Canadian Universities took place, some of whom returned to take up posts in the island. The trade union and co-operative movements had contacts with similar movements in Canada.

The Methodists and some of the smaller sects in the island

Countryside on west coast near Corner Brook

Scenery on east coast on
the road to Bonavista

Photos: Marshall Studios Ltd.

joined in with their Canadian fellows in creating the United Church (1926). Their had been some movement among Anglicans to link up with their fellow religionists in Canada, but this proposal was not generally accepted until after political union had been achieved. The majority of Roman Catholics, being Irish in origin, opposed political union with Canada as they feared that it might lead to their Church coming under the domination of French-Canadians. Taken as a whole cultural contacts with Canada before 1949 were not as great as might have been expected.

The advent of Commission Government (1934) and the changed military and economic position during the 30's and 40's gradually led informed Canadian opinion to become increasingly keen on securing Newfoundland's entry to the Confederation. This was mainly due to Canada's growing sense of national consciousness which came from a greater importance in world politics. A desire to round out her frontiers towards the Atlantic was natural with the growing possibility of attack from Europe on the North American continent. The growth of air transport, both military and civil, made it desirable to obtain bases both in Newfoundland and Labrador. Confederation would also make it possible to bring Labrador and its resources, which had been lost by the Privy Council's decision in 1927, within Canada's boundaries while still being part of the Province of Newfoundland. This change of political climate meant that Canada was prepared to go a good deal further and take a great deal more trouble than in 1895 to secure Confederation. Realizing the enmity that the earlier rebuff had left behind, Canadian statesmen approached the matter with considerable caution being, wisely, unwilling to suggest that they were trying to force Newfoundland against her will to come into union. From Newfoundland's point of view the position in 1948 was very different from 1895. Far more federal services, particularly in the social field, had come into being by the later date, which made the advantages of Confederation appear far more attractive to the average Newfoundlander.

The terms of union, which were finalized after the second referendum, gave Newfoundland six Senators and seven M.Ps. in a House of Commons of 262. Considerable subsidies were to be given to Newfoundland Provincial Government to make

33

good the loss of revenue which resulted from bringing Newfoundland inside the Canadian Customs' system and the handing over to Canada of the right to collect income tax. Many government services, such as railways, telecommunications, civil aviation and broadcasting were handed over to the Federal Government as well as the responsibility for controlling the fisheries. Canadian wage rates were to be extended to all new federal employees and Newfoundland was to rank as one of the Maritime Provinces for transport rates. Help was to be given by the Federal Government in completing surveys of the Province's resources. Control of all other natural resources remained with the Newfoundland Government. The right to make and use margarine in the Province was safeguarded. All benefits from the various federal social services, which included higher veterans' pensions, unemployment insurance, family allowances and old age and blind pensions, were to be extended to Newfoundland. The Newfoundland Regiment was to be revived as part of the Federal Defence Services.

4

THE MACHINERY OF GOVERNMENT

BEFORE the advent of Commission Government (1934) the Executive Council or Cabinet consisted of twelve members, seven of whom held portfolios. Normally the members met under the chairmanship of the Prime Minister, but their minutes were formally approved by the Executive Council when presided over by the Governor. Many members of the Government carried on their private occupations and few looked on Cabinet membership as being a full-time occupation.

The various government activities were re-arranged, under the Commission, into six departments which were presumed to require the full-time attention of their holders. These six Commissioners, presided over by the Governor, formed the Commission Government. The Commission elected from among themselves one of the three Newfoundland members to act as vice-chairman. The Governor became, in effect, Prime Minister; Gordon MacDonald in particular took a very active part in shaping policy.

Some minor re-arrangements of functions took place during the period of the Commission Government, and at the end of its period of office departments were organized as follows: The Department of Finance, which supervised customs, income tax collection and all the activities of the Post Office, including broadcasting, together with liquor control, the management of the Newfoundland Hotel and the administration of the civil service. The Department of Natural Resources covered fisheries, forests and agriculture. Its Co-operative Department encouraged both consumer co-ops, credit societies and agricultural associations. It also controlled Crown lands and had power to create land settlements. In addition it was responsible for preparing maps and surveys of the country and it had, since 1942, run the former Hudson Bay stores in northern Labrador. The khaki-clad Rangers who served as game wardens and as general representatives of the Government in

35

the more outlandish parts also came under this department. The Department of Public Utilities and Supply supervised public works, the railway and steamship services, civil aviation, roads, mines and marine matters other than fisheries. Its supply section had, since 1944, made purchases for all government departments. It was responsible also for the inspection of ships, wharves and wells, and motor car registration, which had greatly increased in recent years. Its Labour Relations Officer mediated in any industrial disputes. These three departments were filled by persons appointed from the United Kingdom. Of the three departments held by Newfoundlanders that of Public Health and Welfare also included local government and social services. The Department of Justice also supervised the police, who were confined to the St. John's area and the larger towns. The Department of Home Affairs and Education also dealt with registration of patents, trade marks, etc., and was responsible for vocational training, resettlement of returning ex-servicemen and supervision of the St. John's housing project.

Like many other parts of North America, Newfoundland suffered very much in the days of Responsible Government from the spoils system. Nearly all government posts were political appointments made by the Government of the day. The Amulree Report rightly pointed out the disastrous effects of this policy on good administration. Civil servants were never certain of security in their jobs and thus refused to take any responsibility. Most of the best men coming up through the local education system refused to consider government service and either sought posts with the paper companies or went to Canada or the U.S.A. in search of a career. The former sectarian strife had led not only to attempts to include persons belonging to each of the three main religious groups in the Cabinet of the day but also to attempts to divide civil service positions equally among them without any reference as to whether those appointed had the particular qualifications for the job. It was assumed that the Minister would give his own sectarian bias to his own department but that there would be an attempt over government as a whole at sharing posts equally between the three main religious groups.

The Commission Government attempted to deal with this problem of giving security of tenure and wiping out sectarian and political bias when making new appointments. Standard salary scales, methods of recruitment and pension schemes were drawn up. After much discussion a Civil Service Act was passed in 1947 which set up a Selection Board to fill the more important posts in government service. The Auditor General was chairman of this committee which included the secretaries of all the departments. It was assumed that technical posts and those of less importance would be filled without bias. The growth of powerful trade unions in the civil service, followed as it has been by negotiated agreements for conditions of employment, will, it is to be hoped, be a safeguard against reversion to the old spoils system. There are many indications that young Newfoundlanders of ability, especially Memorial College students, have been going into government service in recent years. The magistrate system seems to be proving a particularly successful recruiting ground for the higher administrative jobs in the civil service. The tendency elsewhere in North America to introduce " civil service " methods of appointment should also help Newfoundland to maintain the higher standard of government administration which has been built under the Commission.

Outside St. John's, Newfoundland, including Labrador, is divided into 19 districts[1], each under the administration of a magistrate who is the responsible official locally for seeing that the policy of the central Government is carried out. These men, with the assistance of a number of unpaid J.P.s, administer the law locally. The greater part of their time, however, is spent in encouraging local activities, seeing that other government officials do their work properly and acting as a general link between the locality and all departments of government in St. John's. This system of administration, which admirably suits a country with such a scattered population and such difficult communications, has grown up gradually. The earliest stipendiary magistrates were appointed at the end of the 18th century and always had a close contact

[1] See Hansard, 12 December, 1947, 259.
The names of their administrative centres are as follows: Corner Brook, Grand Falls, St. Anthony, Grand Bank, Placentia, Bonavista, Holyrood (for Harbour Main), Harbour Breton, Channel, St. Georges, Bonne Bay, Springdale, Greens Pond (temporarily Glover Town), Clarenville, Bell Island, Goose (for Labrador), Harbour Grace (for Carbonear), St. John's (for Ferryland) and Twillingate. A comparison of these new magistrates' districts with the old census districts shows a big drop in their number in the Conception Bay area (see Appendix 2).

37

with St. John's. Under Responsible Government appointments had, however, frequently been political; Hope Simpson, one of the earlier Commissioners, did much to widen the magistrate's activities and increase his authority rather along the lines of the Indian Civil Service (1935). There was as a result a good deal of fear in government departments in St. John's that the magistrates would become too powerful.

The original magistrates' districts had grown up with the settlement of the coast. The opening of the railway and other improvements of communications had made the earlier districts, especially on the east coast, rather difficult to administer. A general revision of the boundaries of the districts, therefore, took place in the early 1940's, and there have been a number of minor alterations since to suit more recent developments. It can be said today that the magistrates include in their ranks many keen and able men of diverse origins who find personal satisfaction in their varied and interesting work. In the last few years the tendency has grown up to group the magistrates' districts outside St. John's into seven areas with one magistrate exerting a certain amount of supervision over his fellows. It is possible that these larger areas may be made to coincide with the new constituencies in the Canadian Parliament. Some suggestions have been made that these larger areas might be called counties and ultimately given some form of democratic organization. In view of the very large areas which would be covered it does not seem this would be very practicable or would offer any real advantage to the inhabitants.

The magistrate's office was built up partly because of the lack of any effective local government tradition in Newfoundland outside St. John's. A town council had been created in 1888 in the capital and its powers were revised in 1921. A mayor and six councillors are elected every four years for the town as a whole; the mayor has the administrative functions and authority common in many American towns. Under the 1921 Act all ratepayers in the city who are British subjects aged 21 years and over and have resided there for one year, are entitled to one vote for the election of the mayor and one for each of the six councillors. The city's boundaries were extended in 1944 to include the large area on its boundaries taken over for development by the St. John's Housing

Corporation. The city council administers the laws relating to public health and is responsible for the maintenance of lighting, streets, water supply, sewerage, the upkeep of public gardens and general good government of the city. It has no control over the transport or education services. For many years its record was not a good one although there has been much improvement recently, especially in road maintenance.

At the end of the 19th century a considerable number of local elected road boards in the outports were created to maintain local highways with large grants of government funds. The Fishermen's Protective Union later made successful attempts to capture these in order to use them in its agitation against the Government of the day. As a result the road boards were allowed to fall into disuse and were finally swept away by the Commission. Acts were passed in 1931 and 1933 to encourage town planning and to allow municipal councils to be set up in the larger outports. However, nothing had been done to implement these when the Commission took over.

The two paper companies obtained authority over considerable areas adjoining their mills on which they constructed company towns. One of the mining companies also built its own town at Buchans. The two paper towns were well laid out taking advantage of the natural features and were planted with trees which have now grown up and made them into very pleasing " garden cities." Considerable expense has fallen upon the two companies in road maintenance, provision of amenities and the building of halls, schools, etc., for the use of their employees. The introduction of pension schemes since the war has led both companies to introduce proposals for selling houses to their employees. It remains to be seen whether the houses, which were previously painted every three years, will be kept in their present bright colours and good condition. In contrast to the paper towns, Buchans is a dusty treeless mining town right on top of the world which is laid out in the typical American gridiron fashion. The excuse that the mine might have a short life has prevented either the company or its employees dong very much to improve its appearance or layout. Neither of the paper companies had the necessary powers to control the development around the company towns. The result was a rash of squatters' shacks immediately outside the boundaries of the company towns. In

1938 the Commission endeavoured to set up a municipal council in Windsor, the squatter settlement adjoining Grand Falls. In 1942 a similar council was set up in Corner Brook West. Much has been done in both of these settlements to insist on certain minimum standards for future building and to deal with water supplies, sewerage, road building, etc. At Corner Brook West particular difficulties have arisen from the desire of the inhabitants to put their houses high up on the hillsides where they could have good views across the beautiful fiord on which the mill is situated; they did this without regard for the difficulty of providing them with all the services a modern town requires. A returning group of ex-servicemen were particularly insistent in locating their co-operative building scheme in an isolated place where there was practically no soil available for gardens. These two townships still contrast very unfavourably with the neighbouring company towns in the quality of the public services provided, general appearance of the houses and the lack of trees.

When C. R. Attlee, who was then Dominions Secretary as well as British Deputy Prime Minister, visited Newfoundland in 1942 he was struck by the lack of local government and pressed upon the Commission the desirability of its extension not only to provide better local services but also experience in self-government which might subsequently prove useful on a national scale. A Local Government Department was set up under the Department of Public Health and Welfare and an active educational campaign was put in hand to win popular support for creating town and district councils in suitable areas. Where the necessary popular support was forthcoming such councils were set up. By the end of 1948 16 town councils with a population of 85,551 (1945)—St. John's 56,709; other towns 28,842—and 6 district councils with a population (1945) of 5,151 had come into being. Special Acts were passed by the Commission Government to create each of these councils and their powers varied one from another in matters of detail. Most of these Acts gave authority to control buildings, maintain, repair and clean streets and ways, supply water, sewerage and fire-fighting services and to remove nuisances. They were also given the right to expropriate property with compensation where it was necessary to carry out any of these services; most were also given powers to take over derelict or deserted land within their boundaries. Where a town was incorporated and water companies were already in existence they were usually taken over by the new council. A Master Act has been prepared after many delays which would give standard rights and powers to all existing and new local authorities. This would greatly simplify the work of administration and will probably be passed soon after Confederation. Such a Master Act presumably would not prevent a township such as Lewisporte obtaining powers to run a special service such as its municipal lighting plant.

Side by side with this growth of municipal councils has been the introduction of a new local Roads Committee scheme. Starting in 1943 the Commission set up a number of these committees consisting of not less than three and not more than five members appointed by the Commissioner for Public Utilities. This scheme does not apply to settlements with over 2,000 inhabitants where it is assumed that town councils will come into being. These committees, which have in fact been created mainly by the local magistrates, have increased rapidly and numbered 497, with a total of 1,962 committee members, by the end of 1948. These local Roads Committees undoubtedly provide a beginning of local government in smaller outports; probably other services will gradually be given to them in addition to that of road maintenance. Some system of election of a number at least of their membership could in time also be introduced.

The main obstacles to the growth of local government in Newfoundland have been the intense dislike of paying any kind of direct taxation and the economic difficulties in the way of its collection. This long forced the central Government to raise an unhealthily large part of its revenue from indirect taxation. An equally strong objection to direct local taxation has been reinforced by a feeling that any kind of public service required locally should be provided, if it were provided at all, by the central Government. Under Responsible Government much pressure was put upon the Government of the day by local members of the House of Assembly to get public works carried out in their particular constituency. During the chequered history of the fishing industry periods of bad trade tended to be used as arguments to carry out the repair or construction of roads and wharves as a form of relief. The result of this policy not only destroyed self-reliance but made it difficult to build up a healthy local opinion in favour of any kind of public works which were not of a specifically relief character. Many schemes were, therefore, carried out, as a response to local political pressure, without having regard to the needs of the country as a whole—even of the most important needs of the local community concerned.

When the Commission Government decided to build up local government it not only set up a special department under the Department of Health and Welfare but conducted an educational campaign to bring home to Newfoundlanders the merits of local government. When a local council was proposed the magistrate for the area concerned held a public meeting and the proposal was only carried out if sufficient support was found in the locality. The central Government agreed to advance certain sums for particularly desirable local projects and generally undertook to put up dollar for dollar for any scheme initiated by the local council. This meant that some form of local taxation had to be imposed in order to find a considerable part of the local revenue required. By refusing to make grants from central Government to localities which refused to set up local government machinery the Government hoped to persuade the backward areas ultimately to ask for local councils. A considerable number of fairly large communities still remain without any form of local government. There were 14 townships, apart from " company " towns, with over 1,000 inhabitants still in this position at the end of 1948 (population 30,000—1945). The most important of these is Bell Isle, a community of over 9,000 inhabitants drawing its livelihood in the main from its famous iron mines. Both the iron mining company and the local magistrate exercise certain powers there but no attempt has been made to deal with its serious local slums at " The Green " or to plan suitable services for its inhabitants as a whole. It is a pleasant island with many of its inhabitants working small holdings in addition to their work underground. Every attempt to get a local council set up has, however, up to now been defeated at public meetings specially called for that purpose. Bonavista (population, 1,401)[1], Botwood (population, 2,744), Bishop's Falls (population, 2,522) and Deerlake (population, 1,927) are the

[1] These are township population figures for 1945.

largest townships which still possess no form of local government, although the Local Government Department hopes ultimately to introduce local councils for all towns over 1,000 inhabitants and rural district councils in areas where a number of associated outports exceed that figure in population. Once a local council has been set up its first council is appointed by the Local Government Department. After a year or two part of the council retires and new members are then elected to fill vacancies. Ultimately the whole council becomes elective. In most cases the local government vote is possessed by all householders together with persons possessed with some small amount of property. The local magistrate, on behalf of the Local Government Department, appears to retain the right to nominate members of the local council if sufficient candidates do not come forward for election. The local road boards in the smaller outports also raise a considerable part of their funds locally with the same dollar for dollar grant. The larger part of the funds for new building, however, appears to come from grants from the central Government.

All local government powers at Gander, and for five miles around, were vested in the manager of the airport, as the representative of the civil aviation section of the Department of Public Utilities. This airport town, which now has over 3,500 inhabitants, still has no road connection with the outside world. Many wartime buildings have been converted by the Government both for airport use and into living quarters. 542 such houses (380 being married quarters and 162 made available for staffs of the airlines, etc.) had been completed by the end of 1948. Hostels have also been fitted up for the use of unmarried staff. Power has been taken to prevent the growth of squatter settlements in the vicinity and services are being built up for the community, which is united in its dependence upon the great airport. So far no serious demand has arisen locally for any kind of self-government; to all intents and purposes Gander is a company town owned by the Government. Considering its enormous and rapid growth since the end of the war and the big amount of conversion work which has been necessary, Gander has made considerable progress. It is of interest to note that the base at Goose, in Labrador, which remained in the possession of the Canadians, has not been so well planned. There a squatter settlement, at Happy Valley, has been allowed to come into being without any proper planning. It remains to be seen whether the Canadian Federal Government will continue as the local authority now it has taken over Gander Airport or whether a local council will be set up.

The need for larger sized units if local government services are to be effectively provided has already come to the fore in the areas around the paper towns. It was estimated by Bowater's, at the end of 1948, that already nearly 20,000 persons lived in and around Corner Brook. In addition to the company town (population 3,247)[1] there is the original village which has grown into Corner Brook West (with a population of 5,464), Curling (population 1,264) still largely a fishing port, the recently incorporated Corner Brook East (1,914), together with the suburbs of Humber Mouth, Petries, Sopers and Mount Moriah. Schemes are being put forward for uniting some or all of these areas. A township like Corner Brook West, which has been incorporated since 1942, has been able to employ only a very small staff and has been unable to embark on any major road construction schemes owing to the smallness of its income. Bowater's are friendly to the proposal to set up a Greater Corner Brook town council and to hand over to it their local government responsibilities in their company town; this does not meet with enthusiastic response from its inhabitants who fear that they will have to pay local taxation not only to provide for their own services but to make a contribution towards those for the area as a whole. A good deal of opposition to any form of local government still exists in some of the outer suburbs. Nevertheless, the argument in favour of uniting the whole area under one local authority is remarkably strong. The second town in the island would not only achieve a much stronger position in relation to St. John's than the present group of townships can at the moment, but could raise the loans to enable it to put in hand the provision of adequate services for a growing modern town. In 1938 the company town at Corner Brook, when taken over by Bowater's, was dirty, dusty and treeless. Curling is a very pleasantly situated settlement with plenty of trees and green fields and painted houses sloping down to the fiord. There is no reason why the shack areas that have grown up around the company town and

[1] All township figures for 1945.

44

Curling should not also be made worthy of their wonderful situation. Unification of the whole area should carry with it drastic town-planning powers over roads for five miles after they leave the town boundaries as well as over all areas within the new municipal authority. It would probably be wise, in constituting this new township, to keep the existing local government units and the outer suburbs as separate wards for returning members to the joint authority on a population basis. There seems a strong desire that the mayor of the Greater Corner Brook should be elected from the council in the English way instead of being directly elected. Such a larger township would be able to pay reasonable salaries to its administrative officers and could experiment in various ways of raising funds locally. Bowater's would probably be prepared to give some assistance towards building suitable town offices, a public library, or some other buildings required by the new town at its inauguration in view of the financial relief they would obtain from giving up the running of their company town. The tackling of this problem of the future government of Corner Brook urgently requires attention if its development is to take place on suitable modern lines.

The Anglo-Newfoundland Development Co. is also anxious to be free from its financial responsibility for the company town of Grand Falls. The amalgamation of Grand Falls with Windsor, with suitable powers to control development in the surrounding areas, is also much to be desired. Here again, the new township would gain as a whole from being a larger unit (present population approaching 10,000 all told), able to exercise influence in proportion to its size in the island and large enough to finance better services.

The inclusion of the large new estate owned by the St. John's Building Corporation within the city boundaries has prevented the growth of new townships on the outskirts of St. John's. The older township was a long spreadout area stretching inland from the harbour. The addition of the new estates is giving the town a better shape. There is a strong case for dividing it up into wards, each returning members to the city council in proportion to the population. If Corner Brook adopts the English method of electing a mayor St. John's might in time adopt a similar system. At the moment many of the services in the city, which are commonly run by

45

a town council, remain in private hands, such as the bus services and the electricity supply. When the Building Corporation is finally wound up its property will probably pass into the hands of the city council which will then become possessed of a very large part of the city's area and of its houses. An extension of the council's activities would justify an increase in permanent staff and attempts to find new sources of revenue.

The rapid extension of roads in the island is making it necessary to control the growing bus and taxi services. This can be done either by granting franchises or by providing bus services directly. The creation of larger local government units would make it easier for local councils to go directly into this form of activity. It is unlikely that the paper companies would willingly give up some of the services such as provision of electricity, which are already in the hands of subsidiaries. Many of the small townships, however, could easily supply power and light from local rivers if they obtained the necessary authority and financial assistance from the central Government to do this. In view of the scattered nature of settlements in the island and the local supplies of waterpower available there is much to be said for such encouragement. Companies possessing fish-freezing plants and other industrial activities might well be prepared to go into partnership with local council in many districts in creating such a local service.

The Local Government Department is beginning to look ahead and try to create local councils when it expects rapid development in an area. In this way a local council will be able to plan development and provide services as required; it will have the great advantage of being in existence before population comes and thus avoid the strong opposition which has so frequently prevented the creation of satisfactory local councils.

It is still too early to say whether attempts at local government in Newfoundland have been fully justified. The difficulty in getting leaders of local life to come forward and serve as members of local councils and road boards is still very great whilst the opposition to paying local taxation remains very strong. If good government is to come to the many scattered communities in the island, both large and small, these difficulties must be overcome. The strong lead given by the

46

magistrates and continued government propaganda seem to be beginning to produce results. The wider the activities of the local councils and the greater their responsibilities the more likely they are to arouse local interest, to get good men to serve as members and to obtain reasonably paid staff where the work of the authority justifies them.

So far the Local Government Department has sought to proceed by persuasion before setting up local councils. It is doubtful how long they should continue this policy if they are to secure good local government throughout the island. There is much to be said for extending the nominated road board to all outports save the very largest so as to secure a minimum standard of services whilst some of the larger populated areas, such as Bell Isle and Bonavista, might have government managers appointed with all the powers possessed by the manager of Gander, including that of raising local taxation to be assisted by the usual government grants. If, at a later stage, a demand for an elected local council grew up it could easily be introduced. It would be unwise, however, to impose this form of government company town until every effort had been made to persuade the inhabitants to set up a local council.

Under the Act of Union the Canadian Government has in future to appoint a Lieutenant-Governor in place of the Governor previously appointed from London. With certain exceptions, and apart from such powers as were transferred to the Federal Government, the constitution was restored as it was before the Commission Government. The Legislative Council, however, was abolished, the franchise extended to women of 21 and over (only those over 25 had previously had the vote) and a seat given to Labrador in the House of Assembly, so that its total numbers were raised from 27 to 28. No attempt was made to redistribute seats although this had become highly desirable owing to the growth of the paper towns and the shift of population away from the Conception Bay area.

When Smallwood was asked to form the first Provincial Government he created a Cabinet of a dozen members among whom he divided those departments which had come under the six Commissioners and had not passed to the Federal Government. After the election some rearrangements took place which still left a Cabinet of twelve members, a very high proportion of the 22 Government supporters in the House of Assembly. The Prime Minister himself took a special responsibility for economic development. Ministries were set up for Provincial Affairs, Health, Welfare, Education, Finance, Justice, Labour, Public Works, Natural Resources, Fisheries and Co-operatives and Supply. The new ministers were drawn from a wide cross-section of the population. A number had been magistrates or teachers at one time; two were former Commissioners. Their ranks included a labour leader, the President of the Teachers' Association, an active co-operator, some merchants and a lawyer. Some further rearrangement of functions between departments will no doubt take place. Sooner or later the Police and the Rangers will be merged into one force. This might be taken over and run by the Canadian Mounted Police on behalf of the Province; if this is not done the joint service will probably be placed in the Department of Provincial Affairs instead of the Departments of Justice and Natural Resources.

Photo: Lee Wulff.

St. John's Harbour

Splitting codfish on the stagehead, Newfoundland

Photo: Newfoundland Tourist Development Board.

Photo: *Newfoundland Tourist Development Board.*

Pouch Cove (Avalon Peninsula)—Landing stage

5

FISHERIES

WHEN Newfoundlanders talk about "fish" they almost certainly mean cod. Cod, which salts much better than other fish found off Newfoundland, has always been far and away the main fish caught off the island and still remains so today despite the development of other fisheries. These include salmon, herring, halibut, haddock, turbot and lobster, together with caplin and squid which are largely used for bait. Trout is the main fresh water catch whilst seals and whales are hunted by vessels specially adapted for the purpose.

The cod fishery is divided into three groups—inshore, deep sea and Labrador fisheries. The greater proportion of the population in the outports around the coast is occupied in the inshore fishery. Shore based fishermen make their catches from small fishing boats usually possessing 3-4-h.p. motors in addition to their sails. Trap skiffs of 25-28 ft. in length, which are equipped with 8-10-h.p. motors, are also widely used. Fishermen using small boats make their catches up to six miles off shore with hook and line, with trawl lines and, later in the season, with cod nets. The trap boats operate cod traps; these are also set sometimes on shoals near headlands when the fish are running in the early summer. Special decked boats are also used in winter on the south coast which remains open during that period. The hook and line fishermen mainly use caplin, herring and squid for bait, although a jigger is also used.

Deep sea fishing is carried out from the south coast by schooners which fish on the Banks, the great shoals lying off the south-east coast of Newfoundland, although there are some similar ones somewhat nearer the coast.

The Labrador fishery is conducted by three groups. The "stationers" travel up from Newfoundland in the spring to their fishing "rooms" on the shore whence they carry on an inshore fishery during the summer months. Another group,

49

the " floaters," travel up on their own schooners moving up and down the coast as fishing conditions change and splitting and salting their cod fish on board. A third element, the "liviers" are resident in Labrador throughout the winter. They mainly reside during that period up rivers or at the heads of bays where fuel is plentiful and travel down to the outer coast in summer where they fish from " rooms " in the same way as the " stationers." The salmon fishery starts in the early summer on the Avalon coast and moves northward to Labrador. Salmon are taken from rivers right the way through the summer although the best fishing periods vary very much from river to river. The herring fishery is conducted very largely off the west coast; it has become of greater importance all round the island in recent years. The catch of lobsters has also greatly increased directly as a result of the success of the measures taken for their preservation. Caplin is widely consumed locally but little is exported. In the last few years attempts have been made to use haddock, rose fish and many others which are plentiful but have been neglected. Cod liver oil and fish meal are important by-products of the industry.

Sealing is still carried on in March and April of each year although the industry now is nothing like the size it reached in the second quarter of the 19th century. The skin and pelt of two inch thick fat from which oil is made are the object of the seal hunt. Men land on the ice floes to catch the seals which bear their young there as the floes drift to the south. Whaling is carried on both from Newfoundland and Labrador where local shore plants are serviced by whaling ships.

About a third of the population, it is estimated, is mainly dependent upon the fisheries for its livelihood. A far bigger labour force is employed in this industry than any other in Newfoundland although the total value of its exports is now considerably less than that of the paper industry. The labour force employed in the fisheries has declined from 65,000 in 1921 to 37,000 in 1935 and 31,000 in 1945. Of those recorded as employed in the cod fisheries about 80 per cent were mainly engaged on the inshore fishery. The number employed in the deep sea fishery was remarkably small.

During the 20's and 30's Newfoundland's mainstay, the salt cod fishery, appeared to be in continuous decline. Norway, Iceland and other competitors were steadily pushing Newfoundland out of the markets which wars and bad living conditions in the lands around the Mediterranean and in the tropics were reducing. The better quality of their products stood them to good advantage in these years of slump. Newfoundland exporters competed feverishly one with another for such markets as remained; the poor fishermen hastened to place all the fish they could on the market in the effort to increase their income at a time of low prices. The result was catastrophic. Newfoundland salt cod, which had fallen badly in quality during World War I when any " fish " could be sold, retained a bad name in peace-time which took a long time to live down.

Before World War II considerable quantities of frozen salmon were sent to the British market and a large quantity of lobsters was canned on the west coast. The herring fishery, which was very large at the beginning of the century, had practically disappeared as had whaling. The seal hunt declined steadily until the 1920's, where it temporarily stabilized itself before a further decline in the 30's. Little was made of Newfoundland's other fish resources or of their by-products save for some production of cod liver oil.

For the past fifty years the Government of Newfoundland had been trying to build up an efficient Department of Fisheries. After World War I some attempt was made to control exports and prices but such ideas were ahead of public opinion which feared that any form of government interference would increase the scope of political corruption. Finally the depression and the coming of the Commission Government led to the creation of the Newfoundland Fisheries Board which, under the brilliant chairmanship of Gushue, has done so much to rehabilitate the fishing industry, despite intense opposition from almost all sections of the industry in its early years. Up to the declaration of war in 1939 the board felts its way slowly attempting first to control exports and cut out the competition between Newfoundland exporters. The Salt Cod Fish Association, which included all exporters, was organized in various groups according to the markets served. The prices charged in each market for a particular product were settled in conference between the Fisheries Board and the principal members of the group concerned after exploratory negotiations with possible purchasers. Selling machinery was thus set up to deal with the centralized buying that was developing in the Mediterranean countries. All " pinked " and other low grade fish had to be destroyed or sold at very low prices. In this way better prices were obtained in the markets that remained and the good name of Newfoundland products began to be built up; many unnecessary expenses were cut out and some part of the benefit of the improved marketing was passed on to the fishermen.

The difficulty of salting the fish satisfactorily in the damp Newfoundland climate can be understood. The fish had first to be split and boned, then thoroughly washed and salted. After some time it had again to be washed and dried in the sun. This was done on wooden " flakes " which were erected on the shore; rain or over-exposure to the sun might well cause deterioration. Starting in 1936, the Fisheries Board slowly built up a system of regular inspection which did so much for the industry by improving the quality. With the war and the rapid expansion of bulk purchasing in such markets as remained open, the Fisheries Board greatly increased its effective control of the industry and secured the goodwill of the greater proportion both of merchants and fishermen who increasingly recognized its value.

Before World War II there was practically no export of fresh frozen fish save salmon. With its own fisheries largely out of use, Britain asked for all the frozen cod fillets that could be sent her. A rapid rise took place in the frozen fish exports as the war years went by. After careful thought on the part of the Fisheries Board, Dunn, the Commissioner of Natural Resources, brought forward an important Reconstruction scheme for the industry in 1944. Seeing that the salt cod fishery would probably continue to decline if standards of life rose steadily in the countries it served after the war, Dunn asked for a big scale development of the frozen fish side of the industry. He pointed out the desirability of entering and developing the American market which would provide good prices if the Newfoundland products were of high quality. During and since the war a chain of 16 refrigeration plants, using modern methods of quick freezing, have been set up around the coast of Newfoundland. Two principal firms (Job Bros. and Monroe's Fishery Products Co.) were the most active in undertaking this development. The Government was prepared to put up financial assistance in certain cases

52

but little advantage was taken of the offer as existing firms found no difficulty in raising the capital they required for this purpose. A high proportion of these refrigerator plants are on the south coast between St. John's and Port-aux-Basques, but there are a number also on the east coast including the plants in the Petty Nord, at St. Anthony and Englee.

Realizing that the British market would disappear when the war was over and that New England fishermen would press for exclusion of competing Newfoundland products in the cities of the American Atlantic coast, Dunn pressed for attempts to open up a market in the American Middle West. This was done very successfully by the Fishery Products Co. which opened a centre at Cleveland (Ohio), on Lake Erie, for distributing quick-frozen Newfoundland fish to places such as Detroit, Chicago, St. Louis, Indianapolis, Cincinnati and many smaller towns and cities. A service of refrigerator boats was brought into being to carry the fish directly up the St. Lawrence to Cleveland during the summer. The fact that the south coast of Newfoundland remained open during the winter enabled supplies to be shipped across to the Canadian mainland and sent by rail when the St. Lawrence was closed. Other firms also made marketing arrangements in the States, without, unfortunately, always avoiding friction with those selling New England seafoods.

In encouraging these new developments the Fisheries Board showed no hesitation in using its powers to control developments to spread out the refrigeration plants so that they would avoid unnecessary competition between them in obtaining the necessary supplies of fish. It was hoped that these plants would become the nucleus of somewhat larger settlements which could provide the fishermen with better government services and a fuller life than was possible in the small outports.

How effective has the frozen fish development been? The following table shows that the growth of the new industry, which had been rapid up to 1946, has stabilized itself since. This is not, however, an unhealthy position as further expansion in the American market has had to take place to make good the loss of the wartime British market. The high price of meat in America has greatly helped this development. It remains to be seen, however, how far the American public will continue to consume fish if meat falls substantially in price.

53

Such a small quantity of fish, however, is consumed in the American Middle West—very largely lake fish—there appears every possibility that with an increasing population and rising standard of life a demand for a greater variety of diet will develop. This should, therefore, be in favour of Newfoundland seafood, provided that many of the other fish, such as haddock, halibut, turbot, rose fish, flounders and smelts, which have been neglected in the past, are sent to the Middle West as alternatives to cod.

NEWFOUNDLAND FISH EXPORTS[1]

		For year ended 31/3/47	For year ended 31/3/48
(a)	Total number of lb. of fresh, frozen and chilled fish exported from Newfoundland	38,502,955	25,262,822
(b)	Total number of lb. of all fish exported from Newfoundland and including (a)	226,157,025	172,328,215
(c)	Percentages: (a) is of (b)	17.02%	14.66%
(d)	Total number of lb. of cod fish, including salted, canned, frozen and other cures exported from Newfoundland	151,179,770	125,556,286
(e)	Percentages: (d) is of (b)	67.85%	72.86%

So far America is the only available market for frozen fresh fish as the Canadian market is largely met from the other Maritime Provinces. In the long run other markets should come into being as refrigeration facilities develop elsewhere. The whole industry depends very much upon the keeping open of the American market. As will be mentioned in a later chapter, this question of such vital importance to Newfoundland's prosperity is closely bound up with the whole question

[1] Hansard, 31 March, 1949.

of American-Canadian trade relations following Confederation. As the table above shows, the proportion of fish exported in a fresh, frozen or chilled condition is still under 20 per cent of the total catch although it is somewhat higher in value. It should be remembered also that the frozen fish industry already provides employment on shore for nearly 2,000 persons, a quarter of whom are women.

War conditions temporarily knocked out Newfoundland's competitors and enabled good prices to be obtained for the salt cod catch which has remained about the same size as prewar but has greatly increased in value. Such prices obviously cannot be retained as more normal times return. The continued food shortage after the war has, however, been of considerable benefit to Newfoundland. Here, not only has the board taken advantage of the war situation to improve standards but has encouraged the building of artificial drying installations, central curing stations and offal utilization plants. Plenty of running water to wash the fish together with electric light have been found to be big assets. When these plants can be provided—especially if they are close to a refrigeration plant —very great assistance is given to the whole industry and a nucleus created for a substantial settlement. So far progress in providing all these services has been slow, but it has been speeded up since the end of the war. There is, for a very long time to come, likely to be a fairly big, if declining, market for salt cod, especially in the tropics where the human frame requires a considerable consumption of salt. In view of the fact that the growth of the fresh frozen fish industry is likely to proceed more slowly in the immediate future than during the war years, there is every reason for the board and the industry to make the salt cod fishery as efficient as possible.

The herring fishery rose rapidly during World War II and large orders were placed by U.N.R.R.A. for disposal in Europe after the Nazi fall. The export has continued since U.N.R.R.A. terminated as a wide variety of ways for dealing with herring have been developed. It is kippered, dressed and filletted, vinegar-cured and also canned. A large amount is made into meal and oil. So far this development has mainly benefited the west coast and southern Labrador but developments are likely to take place on other parts of the coast where the herring has hitherto been neglected. Much of these specialized products is exported to the States. The end of the war also saw a revival of sealing and whaling. The seal meat, especially flippers which are regarded as a great delicacy, is consumed locally; both whale and seal oil have found ready markets in a time of world-wide fat shortages. Fresh frozen salmon, which was mainly exported to Britain before the war, now goes principally to the States; the lobster harvest has developed in the last few years. Here the Fisheries Board's policy of rigidly controlling the size of the lobster taken from the sea has justified itself up to the hilt. Fishermen themselves have come to realize that it is suicidal to catch " berried " lobsters and have come to assist the enforcement of the rules. The contrast with the position in Nova Scotia, where over-fishing and lack of similar regulations has almost destroyed the lobster fishery, is very striking. In this field the catching of fresh lobsters and their despatch direct to New York and other American markets has led to a considerable decline in the canning of lobster. On the west coast the marketing of lobster is now largely in the hands of fishermen's co-operatives. Some important new canning plants have been constructed for seafood products of all kinds in the last few years with the encouragement of the Fisheries Board. A draft Act has been prepared to tighten up canning practice so as to create a high standard for Newfoundland products. This would give the Fisheries Board powers not only to inspect but to close down unsatisfactory canning units.

There has also been considerable development in the last few years in the use of fish by-products not only in the way of cod liver oil and herring meal and oil, but also in meal made from cod offal, etc. There is room for great expansion in this direction if centralized plants for drying and curing fish are brought into being at different points around the coast.

The Fisheries Board has carried out a good deal of research work considering the very inadequate funds placed at its disposal for this purpose. The industry itself is now beginning to appreciate this work and press for its further expansion. A whole series of frozen bait depots were created in the late 30's mainly by the Board, but partly also by private enterprise, at key points around the coast. This has proved extraordinarily valuable to the fishermen when bait has been short. Efforts were also made to cheapen the distribution of salt before the war. When overseas supplies were cut off the Government organized its import from the mainland. The price was standardized around the coasts and a number of local salt depots were set up by the trade as part of the Government's scheme. Previously the cost of the salt to local fishermen had been greatly increased by the over-centralization of the salt trade in St. John's. With the end of hostilities salt supplies once more became available from the West Indies and Portugal, and the Government was able to see that local distributing points remained in existence.

In the middle and late 30's bounties were given to fishermen for building or rebuilding their vessels. Extensive use was made of this financial assistance which was revived later. At the end of the war some of the " Clarenville " wooden motor boats, which the Government built during the war, were fitted out as refrigerator ships and made available for the use of the industry. Over a number of years the Newfoundland tariff has been gradually revised to exclude from duty gasolene for use in fishermen's motor boats and all supplies needed by fishermen.

Under the terms of the Act of Union all " Fisheries Laws and all Orders Rules and Regulations . . . shall continue in force in the Province of Newfoundland as if Union had not been made, for a period of five years from the date of Union, and thereafter until the Parliament of Canada otherwise provides and shall continue to be administered by the Newfoundland Fisheries Board." The cost of maintaining the board has to be borne by the Government of Canada. Whether the proposed Canning Act will be passed after Confederation remains to be seen. The time has certainly come to try and work out some new kind of fisheries machinery which will cover not only Newfoundland but the Maritime Provinces and Quebec. With his international reputation, Gushue and his colleagues should certainly take an active part in this wider field. Today Newfoundland has gone a good deal further in state control of fisheries through the Fisheries Board than has happened in the Maritime Provinces. It seems quite possible that, with the benefit of Newfoundland's experience, similar machinery may be brought into being for the whole of the Canadian Atlantic fisheries. If this is not acceptable in the other Provinces then it will be essential to allow Newfoundland to keep and develop her own Fisheries Board if her important fishery industry is to maintain the progress which has been taking place in recent years. The needs of Newfoundland will also have to be kept very much in mind when the question of Canadian exports to U.S.A. is under discussion.

6

TIMBER PRODUCTS

FOREST products are now the largest of Newfoundland's exports both in value and volume, although the fisheries provide a larger amount of employment. For the period 1935-40 forest products amounted to 48 per cent of the total exports compared with the 24 per cent which fish and fish products amounted to; in those years the value of the exports of the two industries was about the same. From present trends it looks as though there is more likelihood of the value of timber products being maintained than there is of that of fish products, which will almost certainly decline in value as the world food position improves.

A very large part of the area both of Newfoundland and Labrador carries timber. Spruce is the mainstay of Newfoundland's forest but there are large quantities of yellow and white birch and fir, especially on the west coast. Allowance must, however, be made for the big area of water, bogs and barrens and for the fact that much of the timber is small and scrubby and of little use for anything save firewood. When due allowance has been made for all these factors it remains true that there are very substantial areas, particularly in the valleys of the Exploits, Gander and Humber and along the slopes of the Long Range in the west, which carry very good stands of timber. No satisfactory estimate has yet been made of the timber resources of Labrador but they are certainly also extensive around Hamilton Inlet, along the Hamilton River and the other rivers runing out on the southern part of the Labrador Atlantic coast. At the present time the greater part of Newfoundland's timber resources are leased to two large pulp and paper companies—the Anglo-Newfoundland Development Co. and Bowater's Newfoundland Pulp and Paper Mills. The Anglo-Newfoundland Development Co. controls most of the Exploits Valley, some areas in the east near Gambo and an important area lying along Indian Brook from Halls Bay.

Bowater's control the Humber Valley, some important areas on the Gander River and most of the forests along the Long Range. A number of small companies hold other areas, some of which are exploited and some not. Originally it was intended that all the forest area lying three miles back from the coast should remain in Crown possession to provide the fishermen with lumber and fuel. Certain other areas remain in control of the Crown, the most important of which is the forest area around Salmonier in the Avalon Peninsula. In some cases, however, grants to private concerns extend right down to the coast.

Until the end of the 19th century little use was made of Newfoundland's forests save by the fishermen. Between 1890-1911 a considerable export trade in sawn lumber from Newfoundland existed. Large saw mills were operated at Botwood, Millertown, Glenwood and elsewhere to produce lumber for export to the United Kingdom and South America. By the time the paper industry acquired control of the Exploits Valley most of the really large timber both there and in the Gander Valley had been cut down. The first pulp mill was constructed by the Reid interest at Bishop's Falls in 1c07. Lord Northcliffe founded the Anglo-Newfoundland Development Co. in order to obtain the necessary newsprint for the *Daily Mail* and other London papers in which he was interested. A modern paper mill and township was created by him at Grand Falls in 1909; in 1923 this company took over the pulp mill at Bishop's Falls; the two have since been run as one concern obtaining the necessary power from the Exploits River at both towns. After considerable negotiations a British company helped to finance the construction, between 1923 and 1925, of another paper mill on the tidewater at Corner Brook near the mouth of the Humber, which obtains its necessary power from a plant at Deerlake. This venture cost a great deal more than was anticipated and the company sold out in 1928 to an American concern. Ten years later it changed hands once more when it was purchased by the British firm, Bowater's.

In the late 30's a proposal was actively canvassed for another mill on the Gander River. No company, however, was prepared to go forward to finance such a mill and ultimately Bowater's obtained the lease of most of the timber land along the Gander in return for a promise to expand their Corner Brook plant. Both the two main mills have steadily expanded their output and an important extension which was opened in the autumn of 1948 made Corner Brook the largest paper mill in the world. Large use is made of brooks, rivers and lakes for driving the pulpwood to the mills. The fact that the holdings of the paper companies are scattered means that a good deal of the pulpwood is carried for despatch to Corner Brook by rail, as, for example, from the Gander across to the Humber Valley, or by road as from Hampden at the top of White Bay across to the headwaters of the Humber. The Anglo-Newfoundland Development Co. proposes to take much of its pulpwood from the Indian Brook area by road across to the Exploits for floating down to Grand Falls. Corner Brook, being on the tideway, has a big advantage over Grand Falls, where the paper has to be carried 22 miles by rail to Botwood for export. Corner Brook and Botwood are open for most of the year save from January to March when they freeze up. During this period paper is despatched from Port-aux-Basques and St. John's respectively, although considerable supplies are built up for despatch when the local ports become open.

Both companies sent most of their paper to the United Kingdom and U.S.A. before 1939, although Bowater's had begun finding other markets such as the Argentine just before the war. War transport difficulties and Britain's dollar shortage since have led both companies to market their output very extensively in U.S.A., South America and elsewhere in recent years. Bowater's, for example, send very considerable supplies to Texas and Louisiana by their own company ship which fetches back the sulphur required at the mill. Both companies have been forced by the Government to burn their bark instead of throwing it into the sea and rivers where it was damaging the fish; this has enabled both mills to secure useful economies in fuel.

The two paper companies have widely affected the country's economy. Not only have they created new townships which have become important industrial and distributing centres and markets for agricultural produce, but they have provided a large amount of employment for the island's growing population. By constructing roads in co-operation with the Govern-

61

ment they are opening up large sections of the country and making a big contribution towards the completion of the transinsular road.

To begin with logging was mainly done by the fishermen during the winter months, but it has slowly become the main occupation of a large part of the island's manpower. Wages, both in the woods and the mills, were low in the industry up to the war but have come up to the standards of east Canada during the 40's. Considerable administrative, clerical and technical staffs have also been built up by the companies which have acquired equally good conditions. When the mills were first started a large part of their administrative and technical staffs were brought in from Britain, U.S.A. and Canada. The highest posts in the Anglo-Newfoundland Development Co., however, are now filled by Newfoundlanders as are the majority of important posts with Bowater's. The millworkers and administrative workers mainly live in the mill towns; a considerable proportion of the loggers, however, reside in the outports along the neighbouring coasts where they return when they have earned enough in the woods to cultivate their small holdings and do a little fishing. An increasing number of loggers, however, are drawn from settlements along the railway and from new agricultural settlements such as Cormack, whose inhabitants eke out their income by logging while building up their farms. At the 1945 census nearly 11,000 persons were recorded as working primarily at logging or in the pulp and paper industries. This number has increased very considerably since then. The industry is particularly prosperous at the moment and has made contracts for ten years or more ahead to dispose of a large part of their paper to United States publishing houses; the companies hope that such agreements will safeguard them against the evils of any possible future slump in North America.

A very large number of sawmills, both small and large, surround the Newfoundland coast and make use of the timber both on Crown and private lands not in the possession of the paper companies. The total output of such sawmills is large and meets most of the local needs in the way of building timber, etc., though already there is a large import of building timber from British Columbia for use in St. John's and other large settlements where local timber resources are exhausted. Newfoundlanders are assumed to have the right to cut and fetch any timber they require for fuel from neighbouring forests. This right, plus the exploitation by the sawmills, has already stripped large areas, especially along the coastline, of all timber of any value. The growth of the population has led fuel seekers to go further and further afield to cut down all trees of respectable size. A grave danger has, therefore, arisen of deforestation as seed-bearing trees are removed. To meet local shortages quantities of timber are shipped for fuel and building purposes by local schooners from the areas which are still plentifully supplied.

This danger of over-exploitation of timber resources has forced itself on the Government. Efforts have been made to reduce the number of sawmills and to get others to transfer their activities to some of the private grants of land lying back from the coast. Efforts have also been made to arouse public opinion to the danger but so far with very few results.

The railway has taken steps to use birch ties and to obtain other timber supplies from private lands. By creosoting sleepers and other timber used their life should be greatly prolonged. A Forestry Department has been set up to survey the country's resources of timber and make proposals for conserving them. The largest remaining forest in Avalon around Salmonier has been taken in hand by the State Forestry Department to try and preserve and develop it. Much of the forest here, which had been cut over commercially and left in a bad condition, has been cleaned up, thinned and, in some cases re-planted. Nurseries supply trees for all parts of the island when required and experimental plantings have been made with maples and other trees in the National Park, which the Forestry Department have opened up through the beautiful lake-studded landscape behind Salmonier. Efforts have been made also to preserve the woods around Windsor Lake, the main source of St. John's water supply. Despite the activities of the Forestry Department, the country is far from being awake to the fact that there is a need for an active and constructive forest policy.

The two paper companies have photographed their lands from the air and estimate that they have sufficient supplies of pulpwood to operate their mills successfully. They have put plans in hand for scientific exploitation of their resources so that they cut their lands over again when natural reforestation has taken place.

A fire-fighting service has been built up by the Government in conjunction with the two companies to keep a watch on the most serious danger to their resources. The sight of many burnt out woodlands along the railway shows the need for this service. The change-over of the railway to oil fuel should cut down the risk of fire which necessitates, at present, every train being followed up during the fire season by a trailer to deal with any possible outbreaks. A fire danger campaign is actively waged both in the schools and in propaganda to the public throughout the island. A Forest Insect Survey has also been set up, in co-operation with the paper companies, to collect information for fighting another danger.

Despite the fact that Newfoundland is renowned for its forests a visitor is struck by the lack of trees of any size in or around the settlements. Miles of the forests that do exist consist of dense second growth which seems to make little progress, owing to its jungle-like condition, once it is about 15 years old. So important is the industry to the country's future that drastic steps are necessary to safeguard all forests, especially those which are not in the care of the paper companies. Firstly, such forest land as exists near the outports should be enclosed either privately or by the local community in co-operation with the State Forestry Department. These woods should then be thinned to give them a chance to grow into decent timber. The thinnings could be sold cheaply for fuel in return for the cancellation of the traditional right of the inhabitants in that locality to cut fuel for themselves. In areas where timber supplies were sufficient to allow a continuance of traditional cutting rights these should be limited to the inhabitants of the local settlements. People from farther afield should be excluded and more adequate arrangements made to supply fuel and building timber by water at more reasonable prices than at present. The State Forestry Department should directly take over the full exploitation of forests in the Avalon and Bonavista Peninsulas where timber supplies are largely used up. They should themselves sell off surplus supplies. Such a policy could only be carried through successfully if co-operation with the inhabitants in the nearby outports was secured. The labour required to maintain the forests could be

Corner Brook—Paper Mill

Photo: Newfoundland Tourist Development Board.

Photo: John Parker.

View of town before trees grew up (*c.* 1919)

Grand Falls—

A part of town today

Photo: Marshall Studios, Ltd.

obtained from these outports and an adequate forest protection and exploitation service built up. Where necessary a re-planting policy should be put in hand.

Shortage of money as well as lack of interest have been the reasons for the small amount of attention paid to forest preservation. In many Canadian Provinces a substantial royalty is collected from paper companies which provides revenue for use in preserving and developing forests in the possession of the Province. Under the agreements made with the paper companies, only a small royalty is paid by them and promises have been given not to submit them to any special taxation. The larger sawmills also pay royalities to the Government but the smaller ones get off scot-free. There is much to be said for imposing a substantial royalty on all timber used by the sawmills and for controlling their size and location more drastically than has so far been the case. There is a strong argument also for placing a tax on all privately-owned woodlands. If this was not paid over a period of years possession of such woodlands should lapse to the Crown. This would enable the Government to see that good use was made of privately-owned forests or that they were taken over and developed by the State Forestry Department. All funds received from royalties or taxes on timber land should be made available to the State Forestry Department for development work as also should any proceeds from the sale of thinnings or other lumber from their land. The sooner Newfoundland can break away completely from the bad North American tradition of ruthless exploitation of timber resources and try and build up a conservation policy on the lines of Sweden and Finland the better for her future prosperity. Timber is one of the most important of her natural products and she must develop its production to the full.

Apart from use for building and fuel, local timber is widely used for boat-building both by local fishermen and recently in the state-built wooden shipbuilding yards of Clarenville: it is also used for constructing fishing " flakes " and is worked up by coopers into barrels and casks. Little so far has been done to exploit woods other than spruce and fir, although good furniture can be made from Newfoundland birch. A small furniture factory has come into being at Corner Brook, but much could be done to make use of other wood products both for local consumption and export. Following Confederation a match industry might well be established in the Corner Brook area and use local timber if a wide enough market could be secured.

There are enormous undeveloped timber resources in Labrador which the Government is now attempting to map. The long dispute with Canada as to the ownership of the Labrador hinterland checked any serious attempts at its exploitation until 1927. A company which received extensive grants in south Labrador exported pitprops to South Wales in the late 30's and attempted to revive its business after the end of the war. A centre for exploiting its forests was established at Port Hope Simpson but inadequate capital seems to have been forthcoming to run the business successfully and create the kind of township which would attract and retain the necessary labour force. Bowater's made an extensive survey of the forests around Hamilton Inlet in 1938 and found plenty of suitable timber for pulpwood. There definitely seems room for a paper mill to serve the Hamilton River area. This could probably be placed with most advantage near the airport at Goose and could obtain its power from some of the lower falls of the Hamilton River. A decent-sized township on similar lines to those at Corner Brook or Grand Falls could be built up there which would have easy air communication with the outside world. The climate in the inlet is very much better than on the coast but a difficult problem would arise from the comparatively short season in which the paper could be shipped. Arrangements would have to be made for considerable storage during the winter months and for adequate shipping facilities to get the year's output away during the open season. The added costs which such difficulties would create are likely to delay the construction of such a mill. The increasing demand and general shortage of newsprint, however, should make such development, despite the difficulties, well worthwhile considering in the near future. It would be most advantageous from the Newfoundland point of view if one of the two big paper companies could carry out this future development as they would have the staffs and experience to carry through such development. Proposals for cutting and shipping pulp from this area to either of the existing mills or to a possible new one on the south coast of Newfoundland seem fantastic, although it might be possible to ship some of the lumber from south Labrador to one or other of the existing Newfoundland mills.

Bowater's have shipped a certain amount of wood and pulp to Britain for paper-making since they purchased Corner Brook. Following the end of the war special arrangements were made by Hearst papers in the United States to buy paper from Britain that had been made from Newfoundland wood or pulp. There is a strong feeling in Newfoundland, however, against the export of raw wood because it is felt that such natural resources should be kept for use or manufactured for exports. There is also strong feeling in the island that concessions of timber resources in Labrador should not be made, save to substantial firms which would exploit them properly, making full use of Newfoundland personnel for this purpose. The Provincial Government is, therefore, likely to be cautious about making any grants for their future exploitation. It is also likely to take up with the paper companies and other companies exploiting lumber the whole question of the continued export of raw wood.

7

MINERALS AND WATER POWER

MINING is the third largest source of exports and of employment in the island. In the latter part of the 19th century there was a widespread belief that Newfoundland was rich in mineral resources largely owing to the copper mines at Tilt Cove and other places along Notre Dame Bay, which were well known outside the country. A geological survey was started in Newfoundland as early as 1839 but it had a very chequered history until it was re-established by the Commission Government in 1934; for large periods during the previous century the survey was completely inactive. Since 1934 the department has been steadily built up and efforts made, in conjunction with the most important interests in the mining field, to carry out a geological survey both of the island and of Labrador. Not only has paid staff been created but from two to ten " Summer Geological Parties " a year of American and Canadian students have been used to map the country. Diamond drills have been obtained which have been made available for those desiring to investigate mineral resources in particular areas and maps prepared recording the information that has been found.

At the end of 1948 the mining and quarrying enterprises in the country employed nearly 4,000 persons and it seemed likely that some small increase in this number would take place in the years immediately ahead. The proposed opening up of the iron ore resources in Labrador is estimated to provide employment for about 2,500 men when the scheme is in full operation and possibly up to 5,000 if production is developed in a big way.

The most important of the existing mining ventures is the iron ore production at Bell Island where the various mines are all now owned by the Dominion Steel and Coal Co. of Canada. Mining started here at Wabana in 1893 and grew steadily up to the beginning of World War II. A steady supply of ore has been sent to the company's plant at Sydney in Nova Scotia; the total volume of other exports has varied enormously from year to year. Small quantities of ore have been sent to the United States but very large quantities indeed went to Germany during the rearmament race of the late 30's. Some supplies at this time and during the war went to Great Britain which, since the war, has taken a very large tonnage indeed. During the war itself shortage of shipping and German submarine attacks, some of which took place off Bell Island itself, greatly reduced the output. The future prosperity of Bell Island depends to a very great extent on it being able to retain the British market. The number of employees which were recorded as 1,295 in 1934 had risen to 1,933 by 1938. After falling towards the end of the war to not much over a thousand the number on the payroll had risen to a total of about 2,300 in 1948. The management stated that about 10 per cent of the latter figure would be off duty on any one day.

The ore deposits here, which are not of very high quality, are practically inexhaustible. The mines already run well out under the sea and are given a minimum life of at least 30 years. Mining is carried out continuously throughout the year although loading ceases for four months during the winter. The ore is taken away largely by British ships, which wait in an anchorage off the island to come into the two loading stages. Most of the workers reside on the island though about 250 live in mess houses during the week and return home from time to time to neighbouring outports on the mainland which is linked up with the island by ferry which runs every hour during the daytime in the periods of open water. Buses on the island bring workers to and from the mines and their wives to and from the shops.

The second most important mining venture in Newfoundland is at Buchans, which is owned jointly by the Anglo-Newfoundland Development Co. and the American Smelting and Refining Co. After a good deal of experimenting methods were found of separating the zinc, lead and copper sulphide ore located in this deposit and the mine got into steady working order in the late 20's. It has always been given a fairly short life but has given steady employment for the last ten years to between 750 and 850 employees. Over two hundred of these live in company houses in the town with their families, but about 450 reside in bunk houses. Many of these come for short periods from the outports to take temporary work in the mine. After being separated the ore is taken, partly by private railway and partly by the Newfoundland Railway, down to Botwood for shipping overseas, mainly to the United States. In 1946 the mine was given a seven years' life but new strikes have been made which should prolong its period of working for some years. The management is carrying out extensive survey work in central Newfoundland in the hope of finding further deposits and has taken over an old mine at La Manche on Placentia Bay, which it proposes to re-open. There is not at the present time any difficulty in marketing at a good price all that the mine can produce.

Buchans obtains its power from Bowater's hydro-electric plant at Deerlake. The mine will be placed in considerable difficulty if increased consumption of power by Bowater's mill makes it impossible to continue this supply.

From 1933 onwards the fluorspar deposits of Newfoundland, which are situated in the southern part of the Burin Peninsula near St. Lawrence, have been exploited. War needs in particular stepped up production which went largely to Canada and U.S.A. This mineral is used by the steel, aluminium and chemical industries and the mines give employment for over 250 men. The chief difficulty this industry has experienced is the expense of the local hydro-electric power which needs further development in the Burin area if fluorspar is to compete in overseas markets.

The Dominion Steel and Coal Corporation possess a large limestone quarry on the west coast of Newfoundland at Aguathuna near Port-au-Port; the limestone is shipped to be used as a flux in the smelting of the Bell Island ore and the manufacture of steel. During the quarrying months, from May to November, about 150 men are employed. A number of small brickworks are active on the east coast which meet a large part of the local demand; only a small amount of employment, however, is given.

Prospects in other mining fields are as follows: Traces of uranium have been found and are being actively investigated. Coal deposits have been located in many places on the west coast but, despite exhaustive surveys, have not been found in workable seams. Asbestos, on the other hand, has been found in the Lewis Hills and shows some chance of successful exploitation. The supplies of limestone, gypsum and silica clay in the Port-au-Port Peninsula should enable a cement plant to meet the needs of the west coast to be added to that already opened at St. John's to supply the Avalon and east coast areas. If the price of copper remains sufficiently high, the old mine at Tilt Cove may be reopened mainly to exploit the ore refuse dumps of an earlier age. There seems little likelihood, however, that the old slate mines will be reopened for export to Britain in view of the decline in the use of slate as a roofing material. The geological survey has drilled widely to seek local suplies of salt for the fisheries but so far without success. The possibility of utilizing deposits of pyrites on Pilley's Island to produce sulphur for the paper mills is still being actively investigated.

A much more favourable position exists, however, in Labrador, where large deposits of iron ore have been found both on the Newfoundland and Quebec sides of the border. Soon after the Commission Government took office concessions were granted for exploration in the area round the lakes at the head waters of the Hamilton River. An agreement has been made between the Newfoundland Government and the Labrador Mining and Exploration Co. to fully investigate this area with a view to a concession being granted for the exploitation of any resources found. The rapid exhaustion of the Lake Superior ores in the United States is making it increasingly worthwhile to develop the deposits despite their difficulty of access. Authority has been sought to build a railway from the St. Lawrence River near Seven Islands Bay up to the deposits in the hinterland. Power to work the mines would probably be obtained from the Grand Falls on the Hamilton River. It is expected that work on the port, railway and mines will start in the early 1950's. Confederation with Canada should make it easier to plan the development of these iron ore deposits. The Newfoundland Government has reserved the right, under the Act of Union, to continue to maintain the obligation to employ Newfoundland labour in any concession such as this which was granted before the date of union. The fact that the St. Lawrence River is open to traffic for a much longer period than the Hamilton Inlet was certainly the main factor in the decision to construct the proposed railway rather than one of shorter length down to Goose Bay; if the exploitation of the ore field develops rapidly, however, a railway spur to Hamilton Inlet may also be constructed to provide an alternative port for shipment. Apart from the iron ore deposits, few other mineral resources have so far been found in Labrador. A large part of the country, however, still remains to be surveyed.

Between 1857 and 1946, no less than 4,123,304 acres in Newfoundland itself, apart from concessions in Labrador, had been granted to mining companies for exploitation. The vast majority of these date from before the Commission Government and over two and a half million acres belong to the R. G. Reid concerns. A very large part of these claims are not being operated; their private ownership, however, restricts investigation and exploitation of possible mineral resources in these areas. The Provincial Government has a strong case for imposing taxation, possibly on an acreage basis, on all claims granted for more than ten years which are not at present being exploited. Such a tax could be replaced by a royalty when exploitation was actually taking place. Non-payment of such tax should lead to the surrender to the Crown of all unexploited mining concessions within a definite date. Such an act would assist the Government to encourage active exploitation of the country's mineral resources.

The absence of any high mountains and large waterfalls limits severely the possibility of any extensive hydro-electric development in Newfoundland. The fairly heavy rainfall, however, and the large lake surface produce a steady flow of water in its rivers and brooks. The two paper companies have secured the hydro-electric resources of the Humber and Exploits Rivers which they have already largely utilized. In the Avalon Peninsula and the more thickly settled areas along the coasts local resources in rivers and brooks are being increasingly made use of. The largest unexploited hydro-electric resources are on the south coast where use could be made of the watershed of the Baie d'Este River and of the Gray River. The Government has recently set up a department to survey water power resources and is collecting information as to water flows at suitable points. Here again large concessions have been granted which have not in fact been exploited. The Provincial Government could well pass a similar act to that in operation in Nova Scotia for taking back into the possession of the Crown all water power which is not developed within a reasonable length of time from the granting of the original concession.

Newfoundland's population is never likely to be large enough to make it worth while to develop any kind of grid system in the island. The numerous streams with a steady flow of water, however, make it increasingly desirable to develop local exploitation of water power resources both for local industries and household consumption. There should be a large field for development of these local resources both by industrial concerns and by local government; this could be done in many cases by co-operation between such bodies.

Labrador not only possesses many local streams and rivers which could be exploited on similar lines but has the enormous potential water power of the Hamilton River. The Hamilton Falls should be well able to meet all the needs of the iron ore development schemes on both sides of the border as well as providing a surplus of power for use elsewhere. Any scheme for constructing a paper mill at the head of Hamilton Inlet should find ample water power resources either from the rapids on the lower Hamilton River or from other rivers. In a country lacking adequate coal resources, such as Newfoundland, it should be possible to find all the necessary power required and to save some of the consumption of wood by fully developing the country's water power resources. This can only be done properly if the Provincial Government both surveys and takes control over all water power resources available to see that good use is made of them. A hydroelectric commission should be set up to do this.

8

MERCHANDIZING AND SECONDARY INDUSTRIES

MERCHANDIZING has always been a typical Newfoundland business enterprise although it has given rise to various secondary manufacturing industries in recent years. The merchant had been the mainstay of the British West Country fisheries when they controlled Newfoundland, and the same system sprang up across the Atlantic as soon as the majority of British fishermen using Newfoundland waters had become settlers in the island. The merchant advanced to the fishermen what he required to keep his family alive during the winter and to fit out his boat in the spring on the understanding that the fisherman handed over his catch in the autumn to be set against the debts already incurred. As a result of this credit system the fishermen transferred a large part of the job of risk taking to the merchant and gave up his own economic independence. The merchant, to cover himself, went into all possible branches of trade from financing sealing and bank-fishing, insurance and steamship agencies to banking (until the crash of 1894). In the last half century he has established many small factories to supply consumers' goods for the home market. As different parts of the coast became settled, a number of local merchants grew up who acted as distributing and collecting agents for the St. John's merchants; the latter, however, continued to combine large retail businesses in the capital with wholesaling in many other parts of the island.

Certain changes have taken place in recent years apart from the growth of secondary industries which will be dealt with later in this chapter. Some Canadian distributing houses have opened branches in St. John's and also at Corner Brook, which has become the main distribution centre for the island's west coast; oil distribution is completely in their hands. An important co-operative movement has also grown up, particularly in the west among fishermen and farmers, which has also sought to supply the needs of consumers in most of the larger towns outside St. John's and in a number of small outports. The long-established credit system, although still dominant in the salt cod fishery, has been replaced almost entirely by cash payments in the frozen fish trade. Some of the merchants have dropped part of their activities in the fish trade and have concentrated upon distribution and local manufacture; others, however, still play a very large part in the fishing trade. Practically all the important merchants in St. John's have a very wide variety of activities and few firms have specialized in any particular branch of trade. Despite the many unfavourable criticisms made of the Newfoundland merchandizing system, of its profits and of its undoubted bad effects on the fishermen, an examiniation of the names of the principal merchants of fifty years ago and a comparison with those of today will show that business crises have, from time to time, wiped out many of the merchants who have certainly had many risks to bear.

Owing on one hand to the fisherman's poverty and the difficulty of collecting direct taxes from him and on the other to the merchant's dislike of direct taxation, Newfoundland was forced, before the rise of the paper industry, to raise most of its revenue from indirect taxation. High duties which were imposed in an indiscriminating way on necessities and luxuries alike led to a very high cost of living. Incidentally, they provided protection for local factories which might be set up to produce goods for the small Newfoundland consumer's market. True the tariff was not intended to be protectionist in character but, once in existence, it was difficult to resist pressure to allow local products to be produced either free of or with a reduced excise duty; many raw materials which required to be imported for a local manufacture were also certain to obtain some tariff preference.

The secondary industries which have grown up in Newfoundland can be divided into those which are produced in the main from local raw materials and those whose raw materials have, in the main, to be imported. The former, if their raw materials were easily obtainable, had every chance of meeting local demands without the extra cost which transport added to competitive imports; in such cases, if local manufacture was efficient, there was a possibility of an export trade although in fact this rarely happened. In a large number of industries, however, the manufacturer imported his raw materials and then sought to maintain or raise the tariff to exclude competition from the imported finished goods. The smallness of the Newfoundland market made it difficult to produce goods in this field which could stand up against imports from countries with a much larger home market.

The secondary industries in the country are of a wide variety and are estimated to give full-time employment to over 4,000 people. In addition there are of course the various cottage industries which provide fishermen and farmers with many essential goods and are now producing handicraft goods for the tourist trade. A great majority of industrial plants are at St. John's although an increasing number have been opened at Corner Brook, Grand Falls, Clarenville and around Conception Bay in recent years. Even those industries depending on Newfoundland raw materials rarely seem to be located near their source of supply save, of course, frozen fish plants and mines.

Two worldwide firms (apart from the paper companies) whose headquarters are in Great Britain, have Newfoundland interests, namely the Imperial Tobacco Co. and Lever Bros. which produce tobacco, cigarettes and margarine through local plants. Most of the secondary industries, however, are wholly Newfoundland owned. Of firms manufacturing mainly from imported raw materials there are a large number making aerated waters, beer, bread, biscuits, ice cream and other manufactured foodstuffs. Firms in the above list of industries are well spread round the island. There are no less than four foundries in the island—three of which are in St. John's. Two boot and shoe companies meet a large part of the local demand as also do firms which make nails, rope, nets, twine and marine engines; most of this last group of industries, almost all of which are in St. John's, serve the needs of the fishing industry. Men's clothing is made partly from local raw materials and a woollen mill makes blankets and other goods for the Newfoundland market from local wool supplies. There are a large number of woodworking plants which endeavour to supply building materials, furniture, etc. Brick and cement making also have already been described in earlier chapters.

In the last few years increasing efforts have been made to develop industries using local raw materials which could replace imports. The wooden shipbuilding yard at Clarenville has already been mentioned. Plants have also been created to provide road surfacing materials, creosoting and paper bag making. The local margarine is now being made in part from Newfoundland whale oil. The growth of canning will no doubt place an increased number of Newfoundland produced food-stuffs on the local market both in the way of fish and agricultural products. There should be scope, if the tourist trade develops, for making and selling not only handicraft goods but locally-produced specialty foodstuffs and wood products such as wooden bowls, plates, spoons, eggcups, etc. Research is taking place as to the possibility of using paper mill wastes for the manufacture of wallboard, alcohol, yeast and fertilizers.

The Newfoundland Board of Trade was set up to act as a chamber of commerce before the First World War. To supplement its work the Newfoundland Industrial Development Board was started early in World War II with the backing of the Government and most important business enterprises to encourage industrial development. It has done much useful work in co-operation with the Government to make known Newfoundland's resources and their possibilities. Following the Act of Union the work of these two bodies will have special importance in assisting the secondary industries to adapt themselves to the new position which has arisen as a result of the general reduction of tariffs and their complete removal from products coming in from other Canadian Provinces. Some of the industries mainly dependent on imported raw materials may find themselves in considerable difficulties. There will be all the more reason, therefore, for stimulating industries making use of local raw materials. In this work of readjustment two serious difficulties will have to be tackled. The small size of many of the Newfoundland firms makes it difficult to find adequate resources to build modern up-to-date plants and exploit markets. This has already been found in development of the frozen fish industry where some amalgamation has proved necessary. Amalgamations are required right through the secondary industries if strong local firms are to be built up. It will also be necessary to provide cheaper and more plentiful supplies of hydro-electric power for industry. The Provincial Government, if it is to play an active part in developing Newfoundland's economy, will certainly have to take powers to control as well as encourage future industrial development.

Realizing the undesirability of centring too large a part of the country's population and economic life in the capital, Dunn, when Commissioner of National Resources, decided to locate the new wooden shipbuilding yard at Clarenville which was well situated as a future industrial centre being at the junction of the Bonavista branch with the main transinsular railway and at the head of a deepwater inlet. Other industries have already come to the same site. Clarenville might well also be made a centre for other woodworking industries such as wagon and carriage making and repairing for the railway, furniture-making and wooden specialty goods, etc. The necessary raw materials could be easily brought in by rail or water and all these industries would gain from building up a supply of labour skilled at working in wood. Most Newfoundlanders have a rough knowledge of carpentry but far too many are " wood-butchers." Employment in some of these industries, such as wooden shipbuilding, is likely to vary seasonally and from year to year. The situation, in the same area, of a number of industries using the same material would enable labour to interchange with the expansion and contraction of the work of the particular firms. If this small industrial town is to develop, however, incorporation is essential so that a town council can plan future building and services; cheap and plentiful water power supplies are also vital.

Industrial plants need also to be developed at other places where raw materials and water power are available. A new woollen mill, possibly co-operatively built and operated, might be constructed in the Codroy Valley. Food canning and quick freezing plants will obviously become desirable in the different food producing areas on the west coast as they become settled and opened up. In addition to further frozen fish plants and wood working industries there should be scope for an expansion of soap, paint and fertilizer manufacture. Lever's might be persuaded to develop a new soap plant near Bonavista, which could use whale and other fish oils and export overseas as well as meet local demands. If Newfoundland's wooden houses are in future to be painted as frequently as is desirable to preserve them and keep them waterproof as well as making them look attractive, greatly increased supplies of paint will be required. Here again the possibility of opening a paint factory in the same area for using, in part at any rate, oils produced from fish should be considered. As a greater acreage of land is cleared in the island, the introduction of linseed, which grows very well in similar climates in Europe, should certainly be successful if firm orders and guaranteed prices are offered farmers by the paint makers.

Some of the secondary industries have been established in the Conception Bay area where labour is fairly plentiful and access by sea, rail and road easy. Both Corner Brook and Botwood, the port of Grand Falls, should be further developed as centres for secondary industries dependent upon overseas raw materials. If Canadian firms decide to establish local factories, they might well be encouraged to locate their plants at either of these places in preference to St. John's. On the west coast certainly they would have the advantage of easy contact up the St. Lawrence. It has been reported that a number of American firms have been exploring the possibility of opening factories in Newfoundland in order both to enter the Canadian market and also export overseas to Europe. It is difficult to see, however, what great advantage they would have if they had to import all or most of their raw materials unless they hoped to exploit lower wage rates in Newfoundland.

Union with Canada should certainly cheapen the cost of foodstuffs and other consumer goods brought into the country. The cost of distribution within the country is still ,however, extraordinarily high. Now that the Government has created a Department of Supply to cheapen the cost of supplying the needs of government-owned industries and departments, some further government action is worth considering to try and cut general distribution costs. If the Department of Supply not only helped local producers' associations to market their products but also bought supplies for both producers' and consumers' co-operatives, if they so desired, it might not only be of great assistance to the co-operative movement but would at the same time substantially reduce general distribution costs.

9

TRANSPORT AND COMMUNICATIONS

THE problem of providing an adequate transport system in a thinly peopled country such as Newfoundland, whose population is largely scattered around the outside of the island, has always been and remains difficult and costly to solve. Motor schooners and fishing boats still provide the simplest method of travel from outport to outport. Such a form of transport takes time and is subject to interruption by storm or ice.

As soon as the railway era had begun to open up the North American continent schemes were put forward for a railway in Newfoundland which, it was hoped, would not only link St. John's to the existing east coast settlements but would open up the Exploits Valley, Hall's Bay and the west coast for settlement. It was thought certain that not only would there be big agricultural development but new supplies of minerals would be found and lumber taken off the land through which the railway ran. Construction started on a line to link St. John's with Notre Dame Bay in 1880. The American company which undertook this work failed and the 60 miles they had completed passed to English shareholders who continued a line as far as Harbour Grace in 1884. After many delays the main line was completed to the Exploits River by R. G. Reid in 1893; then the Government realized the desirability of making the line transinsular and had it completed to Port-aux-Basques (1897) with a ferry connection to Canada. In 1898 an amazing contract was made with R. G. Reid by which he was to take over and run the railway for 50 years and was given a very large number of other concessions as well. Owing to strong public criticism this agreement was modified two years later. In 1910 a number of branch lines were put in hand most of which proved completely uneconomic and were pulled up a few years later. Finally in 1923, after the company operating the line had lost very large sums of money every year, the Government was forced to take it over and operate it as a public utility.

Photo: J. C. Parsons.

First plane to cross Atlantic takes off (1919)—Alcock and Brown leave St. John's

Codroy Valley—A fertile area on the south-west coast

The railway system has continued to lose money practically every year save during the boom period of the Second World War when both freight and passenger traffic developed enormously whilst the American and Canadian bases were under construction. Apart from the operating loss a great deal of fresh capital has had to be sunk into the system in order to modernize its rolling stock and the facilities it offers to the travelling public. When considering this financial loss, judgment must be passed on the success or otherwise of the railway in binding the country together and enabling parts of it to be opened up for development. While the roseate hopes of the original promoters have certainly not been fulfilled the Newfoundland Railway can be said to have been of great benefit to the country both politically and economically. Along its track have been built the paper mills at Grand Falls and Corner Brook and the airport at Gander, around which the largest townships outside the Avalon Peninsula have grown up. The transference of pulpwood to the paper mills and of gasolene and oil from Lewisporte to Gander have been helped by the railway as also has the settlement of the west coast. The agricultural areas there will certainly make increasing use of the railway as a better marketing system develops to send their supplies to the larger centres of population. No mineral resources of a workable nature have been found along the line but the private line from Buchans to its port at Botwood makes use of the main line for part of the journey.

In addition to providing a through road from St. John's and the more thickly inhabited parts of the island to Canada three days a week, it provides the principal way at the moment by which tourists can visit the country. The railway's chief drawback is its difficult passage across the high moors at Topsail, which is frequently snowed up in winter. Suggestions have been made for diverting the railway northward to Hall's Bay and then through some of the better agricultural land en route to Deer Lake. As this is the route which the proposed transinsular road is to take it does not seem likely that the railway will be altered to take the same course. Under the terms of Confederation the operation of the railway was taken over by the Canadian National Railways and Newfoundland secured all beneficial railway rates applicable to the Maritime Provinces of Canada. On the day of transfer the railway was in good running condition despite the heavy traffic of the war years. Its locomotives were being converted to oil-burning, partly as an economy and partly to decrease the very real danger of fire which has destroyed so much of the timber along its route. Birch pins were being creosoted to fix the track and the rolling stock included sleeping cars, diners and other comfortable carriages for travelling, together with refrigerator cars for carrying vegetables, fruit, fish or meat. It is to be hoped that co-operation with the larger Canadian National system will bring some further advantages.

In addition to the steamer communication with the mainland the railways run a number of vessels around the coasts and to and from Labrador when the seas are open. This vital means of communication both for passengers and cargo is also run at a loss. In the days of Responsible Government, pressure was put on the Government to see that boats stopped at practically every outport. Journeys are, therefore, very long and many of the smaller stops could, with advantage, be cut out, provided it was arranged that motor boats should bring passengers and cargo to and from the stopping points. Faster and more frequent services could thus be made possible. Great local opposition has, however, been put up to any proposals for changes of this kind. These coastal boats, operated by the Railways Department, have also been taken over by Canadian National Railways. The total staff employed on the railways and coastal shipping system has increased from about 2,000 (1937) to about 4,000 with a growth of traffic.

Newfoundland's road system is very inadequate. Small local pathways or trails have long been opened up between various houses in an outport and between neighbouring settlements. In the Avalon Peninsula roads were opened to connect St. John's with the settlements at Conception Bay early in the 19th century. In no other part of the island was there any considerable system of roads when the Commission took over, although a large number of local roads had been built in response to local needs. In the periods of bad trade a number of these roads had been built as a form of public relief; their construction was frequently due to pressure on the Government by members of the House of Assembly in whose constituency the road work was situated.

To begin with the Commission Government talked about

completing a transinsular highway. Sections were built in the neighbourhood of Corner Brook and Grand Falls to link them to nearby settlements. The cost of building such a highway together with the fear of possibly increased losses on the railway soon led to this scheme being dropped indefinitely. Concentration instead took place upon constructing local roads to link up outports with the railways; many concrete bridges were constructed to improve small local networks. Gradually the need for a better road system became more and more obvious. The paper companies in particular found it necessary to build many private roads of their own to open up their forests.

The number of motor vehicles, both cars and trucks, increased steadily, despite a shortage of oil during the war; this became even more rapid after the end of the war with many returning ex-servicemen investing in vehicles of one kind and another. Towards the end of the war the Commission prepared a ten years' road development scheme. This envisaged an eastern plan to link up the Avalon Peninsula with both the Bonavista and Burin peninsulas. In the west, the Grand Falls area was to be linked with Corner Brook by a road passing, via Hall's Bay and Indian Brook, through the new agricultural settlement of Cormack to Deerlake. Southward from Corner Brook, the road was to run, via Stephenville Crossing, along Bay St. Georges to the Codroy Valley and Port-aux-Basques. Fear of hitting the railway traffic prevented a scheme being put forward for a complete transinsular highway. Good progress has been made in carrying out these plans and a new widened, straightened and paved highway has been completed from St. John's to Carbonear. The Cabot Way links the Avalon Peninsula with Bonavista. Much still requires to be done to improve some of the old local roads which this new road incorporates. The first visitors by road from St. John's nicknamed it " The Caribou Trail." Work is actively proceeding on the 50 miles of road required to link the Burin Peninsula with the Avalon Peninsula. Thirty miles of this had been finished by the end of 1948 and if the present program is continued as planned the road should be opened in 1950. Agreements were made with the paper companies to share with them the expense of completing the road from Badger in the Exploits Valley to Deerlake. This is actively under construction and the link up should be made in the fairly near future, although a large bridge over the Humber to the east of Cormack will probably take some time to construct. In the summer of 1948 the road was opened southward from Corner Brook to Stephenville Crossing. Work has also been started to link Port-aux-Basques with the Codroy Valley but the route has not yet been decided for the road from St. Georges to Codroy, although an attempt will probably be made to carry it through some of the fertile land behind Robinsons. There has also been work on the section of road between Gander and Glenwood which it is hoped to carry on past Norris Arm to link up with the Grand Falls road system at Bishop's Falls.

Opinion in favour of completing the cross-country highway has grown rapidly in the last year or two with the big increase in motor traffic. It is now widely felt that its completion is essential if any serious attempt is to be made to open up Newfoundland to tourist traffic. The same hopes of rapid economic development which were raised by the early schemes for railway construction have also been aroused by the idea of a transinsular road. The completion of a wide, modern, paved highway through some of the finest scenery and best forests and agricultural land in the island will soon no doubt come to pass. The Provincial Government will certainly be in accord with public opinion in attempting to complete this road as soon as possible. No doubt new local roads will also be required to link up with it, and a large number of those which have been constructed to link up with the railway will also serve the transinsular highway. If the country continues to go through a period of moderate prosperity, the amount of local motor traffic is likely to continue to increase, together with the revenue from licenses, etc. The cost of maintenance of this road system will, however, be high and a very big increase in tourist traffic would be necessary if it is to fully justify itself from the economic point of view. Undoubtedly the railway will lose some traffic to the road and the results will have to be carefully examined. Any big increase in tourist traffic can be shared by the railway and can thus offset the transference of some traffic to the road. Long distance haulage of heavy commodities like pulpwood would probably continue to be cheaper by rail and it would also be easier to send agricultural products, especially those travelling by refrigerator car, by rail if they had to go any distance. The Government will certainly be forced to regulate bus and taxi charges so as to prevent unfair competition. A considerable section of the Province's revenue will certainly have to go on road construction and maintenance if the much-desired cross-country road is to be completed in the fairly near future.

In addition to providing the coastal steamer service already mentioned, the Newfoundland Government spent a great deal of money in building a dry dock at St. John's, wharves, harbours and other aids to navigation. Most of these have now passed under the control of the Canadian Federal Government with the exception of the nine wooden motor ships known as the Clarenville boats, which the Provincial Government will continue to operate. These were constructed by the Commission Government during the war and are available for the use of Newfoundland traders to convey cargoes round the coast and also to foreign countries. Some have been fitted up with refrigerator plants to enable fresh frozen fish and other cargoes to be taken to the American and other markets.

Furness Withy and Co. operates ships from Liverpool to St. John's, Halifax and Boston. A number of other lines operate both from St. John's and Corner Brook up the St. Lawrence and to New York and the Canadian Maritime Provinces. The two paper companies formerly possessed their own steamships for taking their products overseas. Most of these were sunk during the war and have not been replaced. A large number of ships of all nationalities are chartered not only to take paper and fish from Newfoundland but also its iron ore and the metals mined at Buchans. A considerable number of Newfoundlanders work on ships of all nationalities, particularly British and Canadian, which regularly enter Newfoundland ports. The British Navy has also recruited a considerable number of Newfoundlanders even in peacetime. Apart from the taking over of the railway coastal services by the Canadian National Railways, Confederation is not likely to affect any important changes in Newfoundland's marine communications.

Alcock and Brown made the first transatlantic flight from St. John's in 1919, but it was not until World War II that the development of air transport placed Newfoundland on the world air map. Gander airport now possesses the largest paved runways in the world, is one of the world's largest airports and is situated at one of the most strategic points in world communications. Back from the coast, near Gander Lake, construction was started in 1936 on a site which, as was hoped, has proved fairly free from fog. With an eye on the coming world war, the British Air Ministry laid out this airport which, it was believed, would prove a useful base for ferrying aircraft across the Atlantic and for safeguarding the North American continent from possible attack. The war brought very rapid development and immense sums were spent by the Canadian, American and British Governments for this purpose. During the war the airport was leased free to the Government of Canada. It was handed back with all its buildings to the Newfoundland Government for a nominal sum in 1946. The Canadian Government continued to operate its meteorological facilities, however, at its own expense. Squadron Leader Pattison, who had planned the original airport, supervised the changeover of Gander to a civilian airport.

The rapid growth of transatlantic air traffic has been reflected in the rapid changes in Gander. At the end of 1948 nearly 2,000 persons, nearly all Newfoundlanders, were employed by the Government, air lines, oil companies and meteorological department in running the airport and meeting the needs of the township of 3,500 inhabitants which has grown up around it. In taking over the airport the Government made it a Newfoundland institution. It was staffed very largely from men who had been employed in the R.A.F. during the war. Attempts are being made to train up personnel required for the various skilled jobs in connection with the servicing of airplanes. The most up-to-date modern equipment, such as radar for blind landing, has been introduced so as to keep the airport up to date. The total cost of running this world airport in 1948 was around three million dollars a year, and receipts coming in from all payments were about two million dollars. The deficit was met in part by the British Government and in part by Newfoundland. Considerable criticisms were advanced in the Convention at the action of the Commission Government in taking over the airport at the end of the war. Undoubtedly there was strong support in the country for the Government's action at that date as it was hoped that the airport would be a source of revenue to the country. In considering the loss, allowance must be made for the large amount of employment of a skilled character given to Newfoundlanders and to the earnings of foreign exchange, particularly American dollars. The desire to take over this very strategic place, both from a military and civilian standpoint, undoubtedly had considerable influence with Canadian negotiators when Confederation was under discussion. Both the Newfoundland and British Governments were also influenced by the desire to cut this heavy annual loss.

Is this sudden growth of Gander likely to be a purely mushroom one? Will the airport decline as rapidly as it has grown if new planes increasingly fly the Atlantic direct from New York to London without a stop? This possibility certainly has to be faced and only future events can settle the question. It seems likely, however, that the need for an airport at such a strategic point, a third of the way from New York to London, will continue. In the first place even non-stop planes may be forced by weather conditions to make frequent use of Gander. Secondly the heaviness of oil fuel, unless some new very light fuel is found, will lead many planes to continue to stop at Gander so as to be able to take a larger number of passengers or a heavier amount of freight than would be possible on a non-stop journey. Such a broken journey would, therefore, continue to be cheaper to the airline than a non-stop one; this would almost certainly be reflected in prices to the consumer. Also the fact that Gander is a meeting point of air routes from Canada as well as from the States will provide a reason for planes of many nationalities to come down there to pick up and drop passengers. With a continued rapid increase in air travel, therefore, it seems unlikely that there will be any decline in the amount of traffic making use of Gander even though there may be a considerable development of non-stop transatlantic traffic.

The wartime port for flying boats at Botwood was dismantled when they ceased to be used. A small emergency airfield continues to be operated at Buchans mainly, however, for local use. Canada retained possession of the airports at Torbay, near St. John's, and of Goose in Labrador. Torbay has been used for civil purposes by Trans-Canada Air Lines; Goose remained primarily a military base and its civilian use was restricted, by agreement with Newfoundland, to times when Gander is blotted out by bad weather. The Americans have retained their land base at Harmons Field near Stephenville and their seaplane base at Argentia, near Placentia, on similar conditions. American use of these bases is unlikely to be affected by Confederation.

Newfoundland should not only benefit from Confederation by cutting out her operating losses at Gander, but it should enable all the Canadian airports in Newfoundland, Labrador and the Maritime Provinces to be operated as one unit. Services to planes should thus be much improved and more latitude given as to which airport was used. Goose probably will come in for increasing civilian use as an alternative to Gander when there is not the strong pressure there has been from Newfoundland to force all traffic possible to use Gander in order to reduce the losses on its operation. More posts for Newfoundlanders will probably become available at Goose and Torbay following new developments, although Gander is likely to remain much the biggest airport on the Canadian Atlantic seaboard.

Little use has, so far, been made of the air for internal transport in either Newfoundland or Labrador. A small number of seaplanes have been used by government or important individuals in the summer months for landing on suitable lakes or bays to reach remote parts of the country. Trans-Canada Air Lines will no doubt further develop the services linking the island with the mainland and a regular service from Goose to Gander and Torbay will become necessary if greater civilian use is to be made of Goose. A development of ambulance services to take cases from remote outports to hospital and of charter planes to link with services at the airports are likely in the near future.

Newfoundland's postal service has provided the country with a reasonably good service considering the scattered nature of the population and the expense of carrying mail to and from outlying settlements, including those of the Labrador coast. During the summer months mail is carried by water on the Government's coastal steamers to most of the points that cannot be reached by the railway or connecting roads. Schooners and motor boats take it on, in certain cases, to the remotest outports. In the winter dog-teams are used for collecting and delivering mail. The difficult periods, when the ice is setting or breaking up, are those in which there is the most interruption of the mail. Newfoundland has achieved some distinction in the stamp-collecting world through its attempts to portray various features of national life and of local fish and animals on its stamps. Complete current sets of stamps were put together for sale to air passengers at Gander. The taking over of the postal service by the Canadian Government has now terminated the long line of separate issues of stamps which dated from 1857. The telegraph service was taken over by the Government at an early date as it showed no sign of being re-munerative in private hands. This proved useful in conveying information quickly to some of the more scattered settlements.

The telephone service in Newfoundland is mainly run by the Avalon Telephone Co. but the Government has been co-operat-ing with this company in the last few years in an attempt to build up a national telephone service. The Avalon company has a good network in St. John's and district. A trans-island line was handed over by the military at the end of the war to the Government, which has spent considerable sums of money in making it more efficient. The local paper companies originally built up services in the neighbourhood of Corner Brook and Grand Falls; these have now been passed over to the Avalon Co. Full use, however, is made of the Post Office trans-island line for long-distance calls. The Post Office itself operates the local telephone service in Gander, at Bonavista, and in a number of similar outports where it is run in connec-tion with the telegraph service. The whole of the government telegraph and telephone services in the island have been handed over to the Canadian Government, which, presumably, will continue to work in co-operation with the Avalon company in developing local telephone and telegraph services.

Newfoundland's geographical situation far out in the Atlantic made it the landfall for an unsuccessful Atlantic cable in 1858 and the first successful one in 1866. Cable installations in Newfoundland today give very little employment. It was from Cabot Tower on Signal Hill at St. John's in 1901 that Marconi sent out his first effective radio messages. Broadcast-ing, however, developed very slowly in the island and it was not until 1930 that the Newfoundland Government began to operate radio services.

In 1949, in addition to a station at St. John's, it also possessed one at Corner Brook and had taken over a local one at Gander after the end of the war. New broadcasting stations are proposed at Grand Falls and at Nain in Labrador. In addition to these government broadcasting stations there is a commercial one at St. John's which reaches all parts of the Avalon Peninsula, and there are some others which are operated on behalf of the churches both in Newfoundland and Labrador.

Half of the cost of the government radio service has been made up by licenses. A good deal of time, however, has been allotted to advertisers in order to find the necessary revenue for running the service. Control has been kept over sponsored programs to prevent advertisement of drink and to see that the advertisements do not unduly intrude themselves upon the listener. Full news bulletins have been given over the radio which has been made use of by the Government to give information thought to be of value and interest to the public. Fishermen in particular have been kept informed about weather conditions and fishing prospects. Many personal messages have been sent out to loggers as well as fishermen and much advice and help provided for farmers and garden owners.

The programs have made good use of local talent particularly in Newfoundland songs. Much of the time, however, has been taken up with gramophone recitals and recordings; the material for these has been drawn from both sides of the Atlantic.

A special Broadcasting Board was set up in 1936 to administer and develop the service, rather on the lines of the British Broadcasting Corporation. It made arrangements to see that the various points of view were given a fair opportunity of stating their case during the referenda on the question of Confederation. The small private station was made very full use of by the anti-Confederates, both before and during the various campaigns. The Government has definitely refused to allow further private commercial stations to be opened on the grounds that they would unduly interfere with the reception of government radio stations whose wavelengths were allotted to them by a body set up by the various North American governments. There seems little justification for continuing a commercial station in St. John's considering the very full facilities which are given to advertisers in the sponsored programmes put out on the government radio stations. Under Confederation, broadcasting in Newfoundland passed under the control of the Canadian Broadcasting Corporation. It is to be hoped that that body will still keep the operation of the local stations in the hands of Newfoundlanders and will see that they provide the services needed by its inhabitants and do not omit programs with local colour.

10

AGRICULTURE

NEWFOUNDLAND has a cool summer climate with heavy snow-fall over much of the east and centre of the country in winter. The rainfall is adequate and the country does not suffer from drought in the summer. The south-east, especially the Avalon Peninsula, suffers from a good deal of fog. The warmest area in summer is the centre of the west coast, particularly Bay St. Georges and the Humber Valley. The Exploits Valley in the north-east, which has a particularly heavy snowfall in winter, is fairly warm in summer.

Much of the cleared land in the Avalon Peninsula has become exhausted through lack of rotation of crops and suit-able fertilizers. Being close to St. John's and the closely settled coastline of Conception and Trinity Bays there are ready markets easily available which should make it worth while making the best possible use even of this not very fertile area.

Patches of good soil are fairly rare in Newfoundland and do not cover a very large part of its total acreage. Fortunately most of the best soil is in the areas in the west which have the better climate. The late settlement of the west coast, however, long postponed their exploitation which is still far from being complete. Thanks to government soil surveys areas of good soil have become known. One of the most important of these is the Codroy Valley in the south-west, particularly the fairly level triangle of land between the Great and Little Codroy Rivers. North of this on the east of Bay St. Georges is a large area of fertile land centred on Robinsons. Some good land also lies along the narrow lower Humber Valley and on the north side of Deer Lake. From there a comparatively large area of good soil stretches as far as Lake Adies between the Long Range on the west and the Upper Humber on the east. Further areas of good soil exist in the

Indian Brook Valley and other areas near Hall's Bay on the north-east coast. The limits of this latter area have not yet been fully defined. It will be seen that these areas lie across the west from the Codroy Valley to Hall's Bay. As the soil surveys are extended some other small patches of good soil will almost certainly be found on the banks of some of the rivers and lakes in other parts of the island. The extent and prospects of settlement of these more fertile districts will be discussed in more detail later in this chapter.

The advent of the soil surveys has made it possible for the Government to encourage settlement in those areas where it has some chance of success and thus avoid the enormous waste of effort in clearing unsuitable land which has discouraged so many would-be farmers in Newfoundland in the past. The generally unfavourable climate from the agricultural point of view on the east coast and the infertility of the soil discouraged fishermen from trying to make a full-time occupation out of the land; those who had inclinations towards agriculture naturally made their way to the richer soil of the western prairies of Canada or the United States. As soon as the prairies had been opened up the cheap grain and meat which they produced came into the Newfoundland market and discouraged attempts at home agricultural production, save in a limited field.

Newfoundland agriculture is of two types—subsistence farming and the production of farm commodities chiefly for sale. The traditional subsistence farming still accounts for the greater part of the country's production. It enables thousands of fishermen and forest workers to improve their diet by the vegetables, meat, milk, eggs and fruit which they produce for their own use on their own smallholdings and gardens. The second type, namely production of farm commodities, chiefly for sale, has as yet made little progress. The fishermen and local people frequently tend to regard farming as a job for their women folk and take little trouble to use good seed or proper fertilizers. An improvement in agricultural practice would enable land already under cultivation in and around the various outports to be much more productive and thus greatly improve their inhabitants' standard of life.

Production for sale has become possible by the growth of new internal markets following the creation of the paper towns

at Corner Brook and Grand Falls and the opening of the transatlantic airport at Gander and of the mining town of Buchans.
The introduction of a flat freight rate on the railway for home
produced agricultural products has been a big advantage to
west coast farmers in sending their products to these markets.
Grain for human consumption and all tropical products will
always be imported into Newfoundland. The island, however, is well suited for the production of potatoes, cabbages
and other vegetables which grow best in a moist climate. Once
suitable land is cleared there is no reason why there should not
be sufficient livestock and poultry to supply the country with a
large part of its meat, milk and eggs. At the present time much
of the hay and oats required are imported at prohibitively high
costs. New grasses have been introduced with a longer growing period, which, with more animal manure, lime and other
fertilizers, should produce better pastures and a larger supply
of animal feeding stuffs for winter from hay, oats, silage, etc.
Maize ripens most summers in the Humber Valley but will
always have to be imported for general use. Greengages,
plums, apples and cherries do well on the west coast and sometimes also in the warmer spots elsewhere. Rhubarb, currants,
strawberries and gooseberries do well everywhere as do wild
fruits such as blueberries, bakeapples, partridge berries and
raspberries. So far remarkably little has been done to develop
these possibilities. There is need everywhere, but particularly
in Avalon, for a large clearance of land to provide more hay
and winter feed for the cows; little fruit has been planted even
in the west and many of the fruit trees in the gardens of the
smaller outports are left unpruned. Locally grown products
available in sufficient quantity and of good quality could
replace many imports of similar products and would make it
unnecessary to bring in so large a quantity of foodstuffs from
warmer climates.

The 1933 Royal Commission pointed out the poor showing
of the country's agriculture. The decline, since the beginning
of the century, of the number of swine and cattle kept on the
island was unfavourably noted despite the increase in the
number of sheep and poultry. The Commission Government
set up an Agricultural Division under the Department of
Natural Resources and set out with the limited funds available
to develop the island's agriculture. A demonstration farm,

94

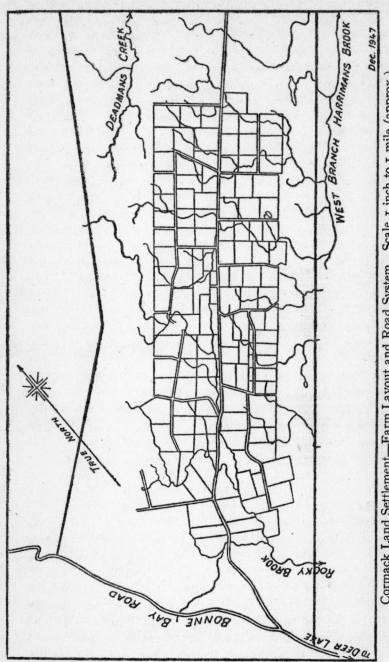

Cornack Land Settlement—Farm Layout and Road System. Scale 1 inch to 1 mile (approx.)

called Mount Pearl, of 192 acres, was purchased in 1935 on bad soil not far from St. John's. 65 acres of this have now been cleared and it has been made a training centre for agricultural students. Between 1934 and 1942 the Commission Government established eleven land settlements containing in all 340 families. Many mistakes were made in this work The earlier settlements were regarded as attempts at social regeneration and the choice of settlers was not based on interest or experience in farming but on need. Little regard was had to the suitability of the soil and most of the settlers ultimately found their chief form of livelihood in other occupations than their farming activities. Useful lessons were learnt from these experiences and were made use of when Dunn took over the Department of Natural Resources.

The soil survey department was first set up. Then the largest unsettled area of good land, which was on the Upper Humber, was obtained from Bowater's. Here it was planned to settle after the war those ex-servicemen who wished to become farmers. Part of the new main road running across the island was led through the centre of the area which was planned to accommodate about 300 farms, each of which was to have 50 acres of good land of which 10 would be cleared before the settler moved in. About 30,000 acres in all was taken over by the Government and was laid out to make the best possible use of the land, some farms being allowed less fertile land in addition to their 50 acres. A large number of agricultural roads link with the main road and give access to all farms. Room has been left for new roads both to the north and south to other farms as the area develops. By the end of 1948 96 farms had been taken up and the settlement had been formally given the name of Cormack. Each settler was provided with a house with two downstairs and three bed rooms, and a room for a bath, together with a barn. The first holdings were laid out for a distance of about 6½ miles along the main road stretching three-quarters of a mile back on either side. As new farms develop the estate will ultimately achieve a width of four miles. Land has been set aside for a church, vicarage and demonstration farm near the centre of the estate, where there are also houses for the manager and staff together with a hall for dances, meetings, etc., a school and co-operative store. Windbreaks have been left along the roads and between fields and

Robinsons — Government bull-dozers clearing land for settlement

Photos:
John Parker

St. John's—Some of the houses built by the St. John's Housing Corporation

Heatherton—Members of farmers' co-op building winter storehouse to keep vegetables for sale in the spring

A Fishing Party

Photo: J. C. Parsons.

three stands of mature timber were kept for future building when Bowater's cut over the area before its settlement. Settlers were drawn from all over the country but must have had farming experience or have gone to the Government farm school. It was assumed that most of them, at least to begin with, would supplement their earnings by logging for part of the year.

In many of the outports the possibility of intelligent farming has been made more difficult by the dividing up of land which has produced many very small uneconomic units. To prevent this evil it was decided that the farms on this new settlement should remain as one unit. Settlers could be turned off after two years if they proved unsatisfactory. It is intended to keep a reserve of land for new farms for farmers' sons as they grow up. The planning of crops and of future land clearance is supervised by the agriculturist, who has a detailed soil plan of the whole area in his office as a basis for all further development. A lime quarry was developed in the neighbourhood and lime has been sold at reasonable prices to the farmers. The number of suitable applicants coming forward to settle at Cormack was less than had been expected. Once the settlement has been firmly established, however, it is likely to fill up fairly rapidly with suitable civilian applicants. It is intended to keep the land clearing apparatus fully occupied during the summer months for some years ahead, both enlarging the area of cleared land for those already established as well as creating new farms as required.

One of the more fertile and successful agricultural areas on the island that is already partially settled is that adjoining Robinsons in the south-west, lying back inland from Bay St. Georges. Here the original outport was a typical fishing village largely engaged in salmon and herring fishing. Thirty years ago the change over to agriculture as the principal form of livelihood gradually took place. The village has been rebuilt further inland away from the sea although its original site can still be traced in the number of small enclosed pastures, all separately owned, which mark the location of the original log cabins which have now disappeared. A large amount of land has been cleared back from the shore on which vegetables and hay are grown to send to Corner Brook and other centres of population. Large areas of uncleared land stretch back to the railway and beyond. There is a tendency for farmers to give their sons some of the uncleared parts of their land and much of it has been cleared with Government assistance for those who were returning ex-servicemen both here and in a number of other villages lying along this part of Bay St. Georges. The serious difficulty in developing this area arises from the parcelling out of many of the settled parts of farms among the farmers' children. As new land is cleared lying further back from the coast it also is frequently divided up with the result that farms today quite often consist of widely scattered fields which are difficult to operate as a single unit. Land hunger is intense and it is difficult to get the question of redistributing fields sensibly discussed. Lying back from the railway is a large area of undeveloped land held by an absentee company which the Government hopes to purchase for future settlement on the lines of Cormack. The Government is unlikely to go ahead with this proposal until clearance of the existing land locally owned has gone further.

South of Robinsons, across the Anguille mountains, lies the Codroy Valley. Considerable sections of this have been settled over the last fifty or sixty years and there are some good pastures and ploughed land. Big areas of good land both up the two river valleys and between their mouths, however, still await clearance. Here the land is usually owned in fairly large units and much uncleared land is attached to that cleared. Division between a farmer's children can thus still take place without producing small and uneconomic units. In view of the difficulties existing in the Robinsons area arising from parcelling of land, the Government would be well advised to obtain possession of all patches of good undeveloped land and to organize their settlement at a later stage, after soil surveys have been undertaken, so that economic holdings can be established which cannot subsequently be split up.

Since the war there has also been considerable further land clearance in the Avalon Peninsula and on the east coast. In the Avalon Peninsula the uneconomic size of many of the existing milk farms is obvious. The high price of milk is directly due to the need to import such a high proportion of the hay and feeding stuffs required by the cows in winter. There is need for a general scheme for land drainage and clearance, following a soil survey, for the east and northern parts of the Avalon Peninsula adjoining the St. John's and Conception Bay markets. If a substantial increase is to take place in the production of hay and other feeding stuffs it can only be as a result of a general government scheme of this kind.

Newfoundland already provides most of the lamb and mutton consumed locally but only a small part of its pork and beef. Much of the pork consumed in the country is of the old salted variety to which the Newfoundlanders became used before the days of canning. There is certainly room for a considerable increase in pig production and there should be some rise in beef production with the growth of the milk herds although most of the beef consumed in the country is always likely to be imported from Canada. In most outports the population decide by vote whether dogs or sheep should be kept; it is not possible to keep both as most of the sheep are left to forage for themselves during summer on unenclosed land. The dogs are largely used to haul in wood to be used as winter fuel. A more active lead from the Department of Agriculture on this subject could greatly increase not only the production of mutton but also of wool. Some years ago a report was prepared for the Commission Government in favour of converting the Port-au-Port Peninsula into a sheep reserve by placing a fence across the isthmus connecting it with the mainland. Much of the peninsula consists of limestone, parts of which could have been cleared to make an admirable sheep walk. This proposal might still be carried out with advantage.

Wool is carded and spun at a number of small local mills in the island and is then knitted into jerseys and underclothing for the fishermen, loggers and other workers in the island. Some attempts have been made by Nonia[1] and other societies working among women in the island to build up the home manufacture of carpets, rugs, blankets, dresses and other woollen products. There is certainly room for a big increase in such work not only to raise the standard of life internally by making far more goods available for personal use and for decorating the home but also for export, particularly to the tourists who it is hoped will come in future years and who would be prepared to purchase high quality goods if of a distinctive character. Cloths of the Harris tweed and similar varieties might well be produced in time in the island.

[1] Newfoundland Outport Nursing and Industrial Association.

There also seems room for building up the greenhouse industry at St. John's, Corner Brook and other larger settlements which could go into the production of early vegetables and crops such as tomatoes and cucumbers which are rarely likely to do well out of doors in the Newfoundland climate. Clearance of more land should enable a far larger cattle population to be carried in the island. If this is to be done, local agricultural advisers working in conjunction with the Agricultural Associations should take an active part in encouraging the building up of herds of breeds suited to the climate. At the moment plenty of horses are available for agricultural work right through the island, particularly on the west coast owing to their sale by the paper companies. If this big asset of the small farmer is to be kept in being, however, horses will have to be bred in the years to come although this does not appear at the moment to be appreciated owing to the recent big drop in their prices.

Such an increase in livestock would help in fertilizing pastures and ploughed fields. The government farm at Mount Pearl and the proposed one at Cormack should not only aim at training men to work on the land but at introducing new kinds of seeds and breeds of animals better suited to local conditions. A watch should be kept on the very interesting work being done in Arctic Russia and northern Canada to develop farming, particular the growth of vegetables, in northern climates. Much of this experience might prove helpful in Newfoundland conditions although the island has not got the resources to do a great deal of original research work on its own in these fields.

Grenfell introduced a herd of reindeer from Lapland into northern Newfoundland in the earlier part of the present century. For some years it looked as though this experiment would be a success and it was even extended for a short time into the central part of the island near Red Indian Lake where there is still an area called Lapland after their Lapp herders. The temptation to kill the tame reindeer as though they were wild caribou or moose proved difficult to restrain and Grenfell finally gave up his efforts to establish a reindeer herd on Newfoundland soil. The great success of the Canadian Government in establishing reindeer herds around the mouth of the Mackenzie with a resultant rise in the standard of life for the local

Eskimos, and the recent British proposal to establish a reindeer herd in Scotland, make it worth while reconsidering the whole question. Not only is there room for such herds in Newfoundland but also in the interior of Labrador where the wild caribou herds have been decimated in recent years. These herds could be introduced with the assistance of the Canadian Federal Government possibly by bringing them eastward from the Mackenzie area over a period of years. Newfoundlanders and men from Labrador, both Liviers and Eskimos, could be sent to train as herders in the Mackenzie area and then bring them gradually to their new homes. By the time they arrived they would know their jobs thoroughly and a great deal of extra meat and leather could thus be made available in Labrador and parts of the island which would benefit all concerned and be a big increase in local resources. It will probably prove far cheaper and more practical to bring large herds overland in the way suggested, despite the great distances, than to bring in fresh new herds on a small scale from Northern Europe.

Fur ranching in Newfoundland has not made as much progress as in many Canadian Provinces chiefly owing to the difficulty of securing adequate supplies of meat for feeding purposes. In 1946 it was estimated that there were 30 fur ranches in the island with a gross population of 650 breeding animals mostly fox and mink. Furs from wild animals provide an occasional subsidiary source of income for many Newfoundlanders. With the improved preservation of game in recent years the number of skins obtained has increased. On the coast of Labrador furs form an important source of income especially to the Eskimos. White settlers at Northwest River on Hamilton Inlet and from the outports at the head of Sandwich Bay obtain considerable incomes from trapping.

Very little has been done to organize the marketing of agricultural products in Newfoundland. Proposals were made in the early 30's for opening a large market in St. John's where farmers could come and display their own products for sale. This did not eventuate as the scheme took no account of the need for storing surpluses of vegetables against the times of the year when they might be short. Merchants were not prepared to instal such accommodation and farmers themselves had not the necessary capital to do so individually or the will or money to enable them to combine successfully for this purpose. One or two large farms in the country have been able to place long-term contracts, such as that of Earl's at Pasadena on the Humber which supplies eggs to the railway, the Bowater's farm at Little Rapids—also on the Humber—which supplies milk to a big distributor in Corner Brook, and the Anglo-Newfoundland Development Co.'s farm near Grand Falls which supplies most of the milk for that town. The two paper companies cleared a good deal of land not only near their mills but also at remote places like Millertown to provide hay and stabling for their horses. The horses have been largely sold off in recent years as caterpillar tractors have been increasingly used in the woods. The companies have, therefore, turned their farms over in the main to milk production to meet a very real need largely among their employees. The fact that they were able to have large supplies both of milk and of other products to dispose of made it possible for them to organize their marketing effectively in contrast to the many small farmers who were also entering the field of production for sale.

The Commission Government encouraged agricultural societies among the farmers which could not only buy seeds, fertilizers, etc., co-operatively, but also sell collectively. The new settlements established up to the war were intended to be run collectively on co-operative lines. Remarkably little progress, however, was made in the direction of co-operative marketing and it has been shown in recent years that good crops in the late summer and autumn can create a glut whilst there is a very marked shortage of vegetables at other times of the year when early cabbages from Texas or Louisiana have fetched high prices at St. John's or Corner Brook. The advent of quick-freezing and development of canning should enable this problem to be tackled.

A warehouse was constructed at Cartyville in the Bay St. Georges area by the Government as an experiment to give local farmers the opportunity of storing their products in a frost-proof building for sale in the spring, but it was not a great success as no-one was entrusted with the job of actually marketing the products which were still placed individually by the farmers using it. The need for better marketing has become increasingly obvious both to the Department of Agriculture organizers and to farmers on the west coast in the last year or two. A successful co-operative society in the Codroy

Valley not only carries on a large retail business but markets local supplies at Port-aux-Basques and elsewhere although it does not yet possess a frost-proof warehouse. At Heatherton, near Robinsons, a group of farmers has come together and jointly built a storehouse with the Government's help and encouragement. The existing storehouse at Cartyville has been handed over to the members of the local agricultural society to run. The settlers at Cormack have established their own co-operative both for buying and selling products and intend, in 1949, to build a frost proof storehouse at Deerlake on the railway from which they can send out their products during the winter. They propose to do the marketing jointly.

Opinion seems to be crystalizing in favour of ten or a dozen warehouses on the west coast for storage which will be run by co-operative agricultural societies. The view is growing that not only should the marketing be done by representatives of these societies on behalf of their members jointly but that there should be some co-ordinating body for the west coast which can accept orders or make contracts on a large scale so that farmers can know what to produce economically and be certain that the available supplies reach those who want them. Not only can much bigger markets than those at present existing be built up in the Corner Brook and Grand Falls areas, if supplies are constant, but there are other possible markets which the small individual farmer has been quite unable to supply. Gander has recently been obtaining milk at a high cost from the St. John's area. All the needs both at the airport and the adjoining town in the way of milk and vegetables and much in other fields also could be met from the west coast. The American bases produce some of their milk on farms of their own but a very large part of their food supplies are brought in at very considerable expense from Canada and the States. If regular graded supplies could be guaranteed to them in Newfoundland they would certainly be prepared to buy locally. There is room also for storage and better marketing in the Avalon Peninsula. The putting on of refrigerator cars on the railway which has been done recently should also enable the western farms to dispose of some of their goods in St. John's and other east coast ports.

The officers of the Department of Agriculture, who have been doing excellent work in trying to improve methods of production, in getting land cleared, etc., will be called upon in the near future to take an active part in helping the farmers' co-operatives in organizing storage and distribution. The Government should be able to use the assistance that it is giving in the provision of frostproof warehouses, together with the inauguration of refrigerator cars and the flat freight rate on the railway for agricultural products, to get the farmers to set up a workable marketing scheme covering the west coast if not the whole of the island. Those who refused to join the co-operative agricultural societies, which would form the basis of any such scheme both among tenants of government land settlements and of independent settlers, could be refused the right to participate in these advantages on the same terms as those who were members. This marketing problem will certainly have to be tackled if Newfoundland agriculture is to be placed on its feet. Every effort should be made by the marketing organizations in the island to get the big merchants and storekeepers not only to stock Newfoundland supplies but to give them preference as far as possible. By making long-term agreements it should be possible to step up local production in many fields where at the moment supplies have to be imported. If a tourist traffic is to be developed hotels and inns should feature local foodstuffs, particularly fruits, far more than they do at the moment.

II

CO-OPERATIVE AND TRADE UNION MOVEMENTS

THE co-operative movement in Newfoundland stems in part from the work of the Grenfell Association which started a number of societies in northern Newfoundland and southern Labrador and in part from Antigonish University in Nova Scotia which has been the centre for developing a co-operative movement in the Maritime Provinces. A society, on the British consumers' co-operative model, had been established at Grand Falls in 1919; this has, however, always operated on its own individual lines. The Commission Government set out actively to develop the co-operative movement as a means of assisting small producers and cutting the cost of distribution. In 1939 there were 34 societies with 3,148 members with a total turnover of $449,113; by 1944 there were 121 societies with 11,216 members with a total turnover of $2,262,210. The co-operative movement has established stores in all of the larger towns and especially along the west coast among fishermen where the movement dominates the frozen lobster trade. Agricultural associations, which are run on co-operative lines, appear to be developing rapidly in the principal farming areas from Cormack down to the Codroy Valley.

It is significant that the co-operative movement has developed most successfully in those parts of the island which are most distant from St. John's. This is due largely to the fact that distances made it difficult for the St. John's merchants to sell and buy directly in these areas and the small size of the early settlements did not make trade sufficiently remunerative to enable local merchants of substance to grow up. Certainly a co-operative movement has raised the standard of life of those taking part in it very substantially as a result of the higher prices that they obtain for their products. This has been one of the factors making for population increase on the west coast and Petty Nord in recent years. In these areas also the co-operative movement was able to build upon local dislike of domination from St. John's which in this case meant control by the Water Street merchant.

The main difficulty experienced by the co-operative movement has been the shortage of suitable managers and responsible officials who could keep books. A number of societies, after encouraging starts unfortunately foundered owing to unsatisfactory bookkeeping and inadequate control by members over officials. The Commission Government set up a Co-operative Division in the Department of Natural Resources to actively encourage development of the movement. Rules were laid down for the keeping of books and societies were only placed on the official register if they fulfilled certain conditions. Educational work in favour of the co-operative movement has been vigorously pushed forward both by the Government and by the societies themselves. Much real help has been obtained from local clergy and other public-spirited persons.

When the Provincial Government took office it made one of its members specially responsible for encouraging co-operation. If the movement is to become a really effective force in Newfoundland's economy, the Government will have to be even more actively associated with the movement. As has been suggested in other chapters local societies will have to come together for joint action in many fields. Both agricultural and fishermen's associations on the west coast—to begin with —will certainly have to organize their marketing jointly. Possibly a co-operative wholesale society will have to be set up for the whole Province to co-ordinate the marketing of local products within and without the island and to purchase imports and to carry on a number of manufactures locally. The Provincial Government's Supply Department could either render a number of services of this kind to the co-operative movement or else assist it in organizing an effective wholesale society. Sooner or later the co-operative movement is likely to come into conflict directly with the big merchants as has happened in Iceland. Once the fishermen on the west coast have demonstratively made a success of the movement it is likely to spread along the north and south coasts towards St. John's. In the first instance, however, the movement must effectively establish itself centrally as well as locally. Only in this way can it obtain strength for further growth even with government help and backing.

Newfoundland labour suffers greatly from the unskilled and casual character of so much of it. The fishermen's traditional form of life colours the whole labour economy of the country. He is used to working when he likes. His wants on the whole are simple and he is accustomed to fishing in the summer after planting his garden and to finishing fishing in the autumn in time to bring in his fuel and potatoes for the winter. He expects to earn enough in the summer months to see him through the winter without working. If he has a very successful catch and prices are good, he frequently knocks off work when he thinks he has earned enough for the year's needs. This same philosophy governs the work of both loggers and miners to a very great extent. Some workers undoubtedly regard these two last occupations as regular ones and endeavour to obtain as large earnings as possible so as to raise their standard of life. Streams of men, however, can be found at various times of the year on the way home to the outports when they want to see their families and feel they have earned enough for the time being. Much work in these various industries is semi-skilled but little of it is really highly skilled.

With the building of the railways and the growth of the paper industry on one hand and of the various secondary industries on the other, new skilled occupations have come into being. Many of these jobs are carried on continuously throughout the year with regular hours of work. Newfoundlanders have shown that they can work well in such conditions when they have become accustomed to them. Newly established industries, however, have very great difficulty in dealing with absenteeism and an enormous turnover of labour. These labour difficulties have been a serious obstacle to the opening of new factories whether sponsored by native or foreign capital. The low standard of education, and frequent illiteracy in the past, certainly has not helped in the efforts to build up an efficient industrial labour force. The British Armed Forces proved a very valuable training ground for Newfoundlanders during World War II by enabling them to obtain a number of skills which have since proved very valuable. Gander could never have been staffed locally if a number of Newfoundlanders had not served in the R.A.F. The railway, Post Office and paper companies all made big efforts to recruit skilled ex-servicemen when they returned. Government training schemes attempted to provide further skills for those who needed them. Many of those who learned to handle motor cars during the war sought to set up as taxi or truck owners after their return. The higher educational standards which are now being aimed at, with the added emphasis on practical training in the schools should help in this difficult job of creating an effective modern labour force. It will be some generations, however, before the ill effects of the old Newfoundland " fishermen's tradition " is completely overcome in the labour field even among men who themselves have nothing to do with fishing.

Newfoundland wages have been low in the past, being considerably behind those of the neighbouring Maritime Provinces of Canada. The earnings of loggers and miners, although somewhat better than those of many fishermen, were no exception to this rule. The enormous fillip to wages given by the work on the American and Canadian bases at the early part of the war had far reaching effects. A strike at the Buchans mine led to an arbitration award by which a cost of living bonus was added to the average wage paid in the mine. Cost of living bonuses have also been added to wages as a result of a numbei of other arbitration awards and negiotiations between unions and employers. As a result of a general rise which has taken place during the 40's the level of Newfoundland wages has come a good deal closer to that of the Canadian Maritime Provinces than was the case before the war. The paper industry has revolutionized the position of its employees. Wages both in the woods and for the factory and office workers of the paper companies have now come up to a level with those of eastern Canada as a whole. This change has been partly secured as a result of the general prosperity of the industry, in part owing to the increased strength of the unions and in part owing to the difficulty of getting loggers during the war years. It should be pointed out, however, that the average fisherman's earnings, although greatly increased since before the war, are still low. The greater the variety of other occupations available in the island the more likely his position is to improve.

The co-operative movement has proved a valuable method of educating Newfoundlanders in democratic organization. So also has the trade union movement. Various small trade unions came into being early in the present century. From

time to time the fishermen, full of indignation against the
merchants have created organizations to try and take economic
and political democratic action on their behalf, The Fishermen's Protective Union in particular put pressure on the political parties in the early part of the present century. Bad times
plus internal quarrels, however, prevented this organization
from achieving all that had been hoped on behalf of its members. Unions followed among railway workers, and skilled
workers in the pulp and paper industries began to be organized
soon after the local mills were opened. As some of the skilled
labour came from Canada these unions were organized as
branches of Canadian organizations. Longshoremen, miners
and loggers, however, were in the meantime beginning to
organize independently. At the advent of the Commission
Government in 1934 the number of trade unionists in Newfoundland was about 20,000. The encouragement offered to the
unions by the Government and the slight improvement in trade
led to an increase of members to about 35,000 by 1939; this had
risen further to 42,000 in 1945. Of this membership it is estimated that 15,000 were in the Fishermen's Protective Union,
which had begun a new lease of life, over 7,000 in the lumber-
men's unions, 4,000 in that of the longshoremen, 3,500 in the
Labourers' Union, over 2,000 in the Miners' Union and substantial numbers in the Shop and Office Employees' Union,
Paper-Makers' Union, various railway unions, the Civil
Service Association and Newfoundland Teachers' Association.
Efforts have been made to bring the various unions together
into the Newfoundland Federation of Labour which is closely
linked with the Canadian and American Federations of Labour;
all local unions, however, have not joined the local federation.
The rapid rise in membership is certainly significant as showing
the greatly improved status of labour which trade union
organization and good trade conditions have made possible
during and since World War II. Union membership, however,
is still very inexperienced and trade union strength, greatly
though it has increased, is probably not as strong as numbers
suggest. Certainly the unions recognize the need for very extensive educational work if they are to consolidate their membership and make better use of their potential power.

Despite the enormous increase in membership and the
economic power of the unions, there has been little intervention

so far by labour in the political field. The Commission Government was friendly and consulted unions on legislation likely to interest them. This was done when the Department of Labour was set up and the Reconstruction training schemes were planned and inaugurated and when the new Workmen's Compensation Act was passed. MacDonald, in particular, did his best to secure the friendly co-operation of the unions in the Government's work. None of the Government's work in these fields, however, seems to have been due to pressure from the unions although they helped to improve legislation for regularizing conditions in logging camps, in shops and in mines. Interest in the activities of the British Labour Party led to the creation of a Newfoundland Labour Party when discussions were taking place which led to the calling of the National Convention. Members were elected to that body for the Humber District and Bell Island on a specifically Labour ticket. When the Convention met, however, they took different sides on the Confederation issue. In the first provincial election some prominent trade unionists backed the Progressive Conservatives although the majority of active unionists outside the capital supported Smallwood's Liberals. So far there is no evidence that any considerable part of either the unions' membership or officials have seriously thought of building up a Labour Party with a distinctive policy aiming at capturing control of the Provincial Government.

12

TOURISM

BEFORE World War II Newfoundland's tourist industry was on a very small scale. A small number of fairly well-to-do sportsmen visited the island to take advantage of its amazing salmon rivers and to shoot an occasional moose or caribou. They mainly visited the west coast and were prepared to rough it, staying in not very comfortable log cabins in the forests near their fishing pools. Such visitors spent a good deal of money per head but were few in number and revelled in the remoteness and difficulty of access of the places they visited. In addition there were a considerable number of passengers on cruises who stopped off at St. John's and one or two other points on the coast for short periods during their vacation. The absence of roads made it difficult for visitors to travel extensively in the island and only a small number availed themselves of travelling facilities on the railway or coastal steamers. In addition to these visitors, most of whom were Americans, there were also a considerable number of Newfoundlanders, who had taken up their residence in Canada or the United States, and who came home to spend a holiday at their birthplaces, usually with relatives. They also made a considerable contribution economically to their country of origin.

World War II and the changes which have followed have altered the situation. Firstly, many among the very considerable number both of Canadians and Americans who came to occupy the bases during the war became attached to the country, were anxious to return for holidays and have made its charms known to friends. Secondly, the development of air travel has made it easy for transatlantic passengers to stop off to visit the country or for those wishing to come there only for a holiday to do so far more speedily than they could in the past. Cruises have once more been resumed and the railway is much better fitted to deal with holiday traffic than was the case before the war. In the holiday months berths on the train are now booked up well in advance. This traffic in the main wishes to fish and shoot but there are an increasing number who appreciate the excellent scenery of the country's west coast and find the outports, with their painted houses and sailing vessels picturesque and interesting.

As the war drew towards its close a good deal of discussion took place in the island about the possibility of developing the country's tourist trade and a number of reports were prepared on the matter. The Commission Government, however, did not feel that they could spend any considerable sums of money in developing the tourist trade with the result that those persons who had voluntarily agreed to serve on the Tourist Development Board lost interest and resigned their positions.

The Provincial Government will have to tackle the whole question of creating a tourist industry almost from scratch if this important potential source of wealth to Newfoundland is to be effectively developed. The industry will never get anywhere if it is just left to come into being on its own. A policy needs to be worked out to build up this industry over a number of years if results are to be really worth while. To do this a Ministry of Tourism needs to be created to prepare such a plan and to be a driving force for carrying it out. If such a plan is to be carried out account must be taken of Newfoundland's present advantages and disadvantages from this standpoint. The country has some important assets. In the summer months when much of the American Continent is dried up and sweltering in the heat the island is far enough north with the sea on all sides not to be too hot. Its natural scenery of mountains (on the west coast), lakes, bays and rugged coastline is attractive and the bright green meadows round the outports contrast admirably with the surrounding dark green spruce forests and grey-blue of the sea. Most of the country is free from the fog which is widely and wrongly believed to descend frequently upon it. With easier communications more visitors would come for the salmon fishing and shooting. Much has been done, and more can be done, to see that the rivers remain well-stocked and game is available for visitors as well as residents. The Government has forced the paper companies to burn their bark instead of throwing it into the rivers. This action, in conjunction with the building of ladders for salmon at waterfalls has greatly improved river fishing. Game wardens with the assist-

Photo: Marshall Studios Ltd.

Lomond (Bonne Bay)—an outport on the west coast

Grand Falls—High School

Photo: Marshall Studios Ltd.

St. John's—View from Signal Hill

Photo: Fox.

ance of the Rangers, thanks to the Game Laws, have been building up the numbers of Newfoundland's wild animals and game. The beaver, once practically extinct, can now again be seen in many parts of the island. A survey of suitable rivers and lakes for fishing needs to be made and plans prepared to see that an adequate number of guides and cabins are available. The local magistrates, acting as agents for the Ministry of Tourism, could take the initiative in getting local people to supply these services where they were not yet present.

No big scale development of tourist traffic can take place, however, until the transinsular road has been completed with suitable side roads to the more important and interesting outports. Many Americans would regard Newfoundland as an " ultima Thule " to be visited if they could cross over and explore it with their cars. Once the road is completed across the island boats could bring over cars to either Port-aux-Basques or Corner Brook on the west coast, or to St. John's on the east. The opening up of the road only on the west from Botwood to Port-aux-Basques would make it possible for tourists to visit the most interesting part of the country. Full benefit to the tourist traffic, however, will only come with the completion of the road right across the island. It should be one of the urgent jobs of the Ministry of Tourism to press for the completion of the transinsular road as soon as possible.

In building the road, which will take some years to complete, there is need continually to have in mind its future use by tourists. Not only should it be well laid out to take tourist traffic but rigid rules need to be laid down and enforced to control development along its borders. Firstly, no houses should be allowed to be constructed along this road without permission. It will be tragic if a line of shacks is allowed to grow up, hoping to serve tourists but in fact spoiling the scenery. Plans for gas stations and places for refreshments ought to be approved by the Ministry of Tourism before being allowed to be carried out. Would-be squatters should be made to settle in villages and to build decent houses. Advertisements should be rigidly controlled not only along the main road but in all villages and open country if the beauty of Newfoundland's scenery is to be appreciated by the tourist. Some years ago the housewives of Honolulu combined together to clean up that beautiful island by removing ugly wayside advertisements. Coca Cola advertisements are already very prominent in a number of Newfoundland outports. If the tourist is to be encouraged to come so far north he must find better scenery than an advertisement-bound main road in the American Middle-West.

Newfoundland scenery has a natural charm but it has not the startling grandeur of the Rockies. Like the beauty of the English countryside, much of its charm is already man-made —and man can make it very much more beautiful than it already is—or spoil it. Newfoundland suffers very much from an absence of large trees anywhere near human settlements— a fact which surprises and impresses unfavourably a tourist to this land renowned for its forests. This is due to the cutting down by the inhabitants of all trees of any size for either lumber or fuel. In this lack of large trees the Newfoundland outport of 1950 closely resembles the English village of 1750 for the same reasons. Large timber near human settlements only came into existence in Britain as a result of definite planting of trees and of the enclosure and preservation of woodlands. The enclosure and thinning of woodlands near settlements— and in the Avalon Peninsula generally—is desirable not only from the point of view of proper forest exploitation but also from that of creating amenities which will definitely add to the scenic character of the country. The effects of tree planting in the company towns of Corner Brook and Grand Falls shows what can be done. The Government should encourage individuals and town councils to plant fruit trees where they will grow, flowering shrubs like lilac and decorative trees such as poplars, birches and dogwood (mountain ash) in their gardens and in suitable corners of land adjoining public streets. Along the transinsular road, particularly in cuttings or on embankments, groups of trees should be planted to set off the natural scenery. In particular regard should be had to those which would look well during the summer period when tourists are travelling about the country. Use could certainly be made of the small local maple whose leaves go a bright scarlet in early September and to the dogwood whose clusters of red berries look like masses of scarlet blossom. Such trees would, of course, require to be fenced when first planted. If this were done as the transinsular road were built they would become established before the arrival of any very large numbers of tourists.

A more difficult problem is created by the need to plant a number of trees in St. John's where the inhabitants of the waterfront would certainly be tempted to tear them down for fuel. A number exist up the Waterford Valley behind the town and they are being planted in the new housing estates. The gradual disappearance of trees from the slope on the east side of the harbour is leading to rapid erosion of the soil which is washed down in times of heavy rainfall upon the houses beneath. Schemes for enclosing and planting part of these slopes would help to prevent a recurrence of such misfortunes as well as add to the beauty of the town's surroundings. Most foreign tourists to St. John's climb Signal Hill to see a wonderful view of the town from Cabot's Tower. A number of trees could certainly with advantage be planted on the approaches to the hill and the view over the town would be much improved if a few groups of poplars and birches could be seen near the cathedrals, and in some other parts of the town. If trees are to get established anywhere near St. John's, it will be necessary to do a good deal of education of the public. The experience of George Lansbury, the East London Labour leader, is worth considering. His first efforts to plant trees in the slummy streets of Poplar were a complete failure as they were all torn down by the school children. He then went round to each school, explained that he proposed to plant trees in its immediate neighbourhood and asked for volunteers from among the older boys to form clubs to protect them and look after them. At the end of World War II many streets in Poplar could be seen with the houses all demolished by the blitz but with the trees still flourishing. St. John's has a fine site and its appearance from Signal Hill—as well as within the town itself—would be much improved if some more trees could be established.

As has already been mentioned in other chapters, a typical Newfoundland outport looks very attractive when its wooden houses are in good repair and are brightly painted. This should be definitely encouraged by the Government not only to improve the amenities of the inhabitants but also because the tourist to the country wants to see places that look gay and cheerful and not looking broken down and slummy. The Government and local authorities could give a lead by seeing that all their own buildings are repainted at regular intervals, say once every third year. Much of the railway property has been painted in cream and green. Other departments could use other distinctive colours. The Ministry of Tourism could certainly take the initiative in this matter in approaching the Federal Government and the large stores to see if colour schemes could be agreed and the painting done regularly. An intensely ugly waterproofing material made to imitate brickwork has been introduced recently to tack over woodwork. This obvious sham should be prohibited by law if villages are to maintain their pleasant appearance. It would be important also to see that garages, gas stations and refreshment houses were each individually painted distinctive colours and not allowed to look cheap and garish. Historical buildings and sites should be scheduled, put into good condition and opened to the public. If necessary they should be taken over by the Ministry of Tourism. Many need to be dealt with soon if they are not to be lost. I found the field from which Alcock and Brown made the first flight across the Atlantic in a very neglected condition; it would make an excellent playing field. The Ministry of Tourism could also take responsibility for seeing that the roads were well sign-posted. Yellow road signs with black lettering of place names, which are a distinctive feature of the German roads, might be introduced. They should show up well both in the summer and winter. Parts of the island are disfigured by dumps of old metal made up of old containers and decaying motor cars. I noticed particularly large amounts of such debris along the railway near Buchans and about the townships of Gander and Botwood. The Government could organize a " spring cleaning " campaign right through the country and encourage local authorities, where they exist, to deal with such nuisances.

Newfoundland is very lacking in hotels apart from the large " Newfoundland Hotel " in St. John's which is government-owned. This is an unfortunate name as it suggests to the visitor that it is practically the only hotel in the island. It would be a good idea to rename it the " Fort William " hotel as it is built on its site. The Ministry of Tourism could take the initiative in planning the opening of hotels and inns to serve all parts of the island likely to be visited by tourists, particularly along the new main road down the west coast and in the Avalon Peninsula. In certain cases the Government might be prepared to hold a certain number of shares in such hotels or inns to help them get established. Many of these might be started in a small way in the immediate future with the idea of being extended as tourist traffic justified it.

If a tourist trade is to be built up in Newfoundland the country's drink laws will have to be drastically overhauled. A small number of so-called tourist hotels and beer taverns exist, mainly in the Avalon Peninsula. All these are now closed on Sundays and their hours on other days are restricted. It is true that little use has so far been made of them by tourists but a system of hotels where drink can be taken in comfort under decent conditions must be brought into being if visitors are to feel at home. The State Liquor Control controls all sales of rum, the principal national alcoholic drink, other spirits, wines, etc. The fisherman wanting a drink is unable to obtain anything less than a complete bottle with the result that, when he has the opportunity, he buys one, drinks the whole of it right off standing up and then collapses in a nearby doorway. The encouragement of clubs and taverns where beer and non-alcoholic drinks alone were consumed, provided conditions were decent, would be one way of meeting this problem. The granting of permits to hotels for selling beer, rum and other drinks would enable the Ministry of Tourism to insist on a minimum standard of bedroom, dining room and lounge accommodation. If necessary the Swedish custom could be adopted of allowing visitors staying or taking meals to obtain drinks more easily than residents in the neighbourhood. From a social point of view, however, it is desirable that Newfoundlanders should be treated as responsible adults as soon as possible and allowed to obtain drinks under responsible conditions. The State Liquor Control could still act as importer and wholesaler for the hotels as well as continue to retail direct from its own stores as it now does in St. John's and Corner Brook. It might also take over the local breweries if it wished to strengthen its control of the drink trade; it could also produce a good quality spruce beer for sale to tourists to supplement the existing homemade products.

The meals provided on the railway and in the principal hotels are certainly up to the average American standard. The railway makes a point of always supplying salmon or some other local fish as one of the principal courses in a meal.

Apart from this little is done to give the menus local character. The greater number of tourists are always likely to come from the United States and it is, therefore, essential that the menus should frequently include the inevitable steak, fried chicken and other dishes which Americans favour. A large number of Americans, however, who take the trouble to visit the island want something a little different to what they are accustomed. The Ministry of Tourism should, therefore, encourage hotels to make a specialty of good local dishes. It would be a good idea if the Newfoundland Hotel, the railway and other important places of refreshment could be encouraged to make a specialty of a Tastyboard on the lines of the Scandinavian Smorgasbord which could make a good dislay of local fish and other dishes such as venison. Local firms undoubtedly could be persuaded to co-operate in preparing canned goods for such a display; this would supply them with an opportunity of getting some of them known so that they could be exported. In any case the local lamb and pork would make excellent hot dishes and blueberries and other locally-produced fruits, both wild and cultivated, could form the basis of ices and sundaes or of fruit juices.

The breeding of Newfoundland and Labrador dogs for sale to tourists could also be encouraged. In the last few years the paper towns have organized successful fairs and festivals for the display of local products and the encouragement of local talent especially in Newfoundland's songs and dances. These should be more widespread and should be timed so that they could be worked into the end of the tourist season.

There is a great danger of Newfoundlanders trying to Americanize everything in connection with the tourist industry with the idea that they will thereby attract American visitors. This would be a very big misake. Americans certainly want as far as possible all the comfort they are used to in the way of clean beds, satisfactory sanitary arrangements, comfortable motor cars, etc. They also want to be able to obtain the foods to which they are accustomed reasonably often. They do not, however, want to find Newfoundland to be just a northern extension of the Middle West. When they visit French Canada or Europe they are particularly attracted by what is different from their home country. It is important, therefore, for those responsible for Newfoundland's tourist development to do their best to maintain or give a distinctive Newfoundland character to those things with which the tourists come into contact. The scene in the outports, therefore, should look distinctive. New buildings should not be made to look like those in a Middle Western town. Americans should be given the opportunity of escaping from advertisements. Local products, especially food, handicraft goods, local songs and dances and customs, even local accents should be encouraged and made the most of. Unless Americans find Newfoundland distinctive in national character and scenery they will not take the trouble to travel so far afield, particularly when they have the very distinctive French Canada much closer at hand.

So important potentially is the tourist industry as a way of raising the standard of life of the country that a Ministry of Tourism should certainly be set up by the Provincial Government to watch all developments in the national economy to see that their effects will assist the industry's future development. Other Canadian Provincial Governments have taken an active part in building up this trade and there is no reason why Newfoundland should not do the same with even greater energy.

13

EDUCATION AND HOUSING

SCHOOLS in Newfoundland were first established by the churches and were usually run by the local clergy. Grants-in-aid were given in 1836 by the Government to support local School Boards which include clergy of all denominations; owing to friction, separate Catholic and Anglican Boards were set up in 1843. As other sects got organized and made converts further difficulties arose and, in 1874, it was agreed that School Boards should be created for each important denomination wherever it had strong local support. A Central Education Committee was set up at the same time which included representatives of the three most important denominations (Anglicans, Catholics and Methodists). Until 1909 all schools were erected with Church funds which were raised in the different localities. The two paper companies constructed common schools of an undenominational character in their company towns; the Catholics, however, refused to recognize these and later provided their own schools in these towns. The Grenfell Mission also created undenominational schools at St. Anthony and in the southern part of Labrador. The Methodists and later the United Church from time to time supported proposals for setting up a general system of undenominational schools for non-Catholics. This did not meet with any support from the Anglicans and a large proportion of their own supporters continued to prefer a denominational system.

The Act of 1874 had laid it down that children should not have to attend religious teaching in a denominational school if their parents did not wish them to do so. This understanding between the Churches has been generally honoured. Co-operation was shown in the creation of the Council of Higher Education in 1893 which drew up the main curriculum, synopsis and system of examination for the older children. There was, also, agreement between the denominations in setting up the Memorial University College in 1925. At the establishment of the Commission Government in 1934 the education system still left much to be desired. Elementary education was not compulsory even in the settlements where there were schools and a large part of the population was illiterate. Many of the school buildings consisted only of one room and were frequently in a very bad condition; teachers were inadequately paid.

In the early days of Commission Government many criticisms were made of the denominational system. There was a good deal of talk of trying to change it. The wastage of having a number of rival denominational schools in one small settlement when others were not properly served was pointed out to all. I was myself very struck by the many denominational schools serving Botwood when first visiting that settlement. In fact, however, a very large proportion of the population in different outports tended to belong to one particular Church which had made itself responsible for constructing the local school. As a result of a survey made in 1944, it was shown that 25 per cent of the schools in the country were involved in denominational duplication; only 12.8 per cent of the actual school places in the country, however, were involved. These figures made no allowance for the fact that the larger settlements would certainly require more than one school in any case and many of the others were spread out in such a way as to make more than one school desirable if children were to be able to attend reasonably easily in the winter months.

There has been some growth, under the Commission Government, in the number of children attending common schools. They have been set up in some of the new land settlements created before the war and at Cormack since. They have continued to be a feature of the paper towns and have also come into being at Gander. Recently the Salvation Army have backed the general public demand for extension of common schools to meet the educational needs in Corner Brook West and district. The Grenfell Mission have continued to expand their educational facilities on these lines in the areas they serve. In 1946, however, the total percentage of children attending such schools only amounted to 7 per cent.

Some small increase in public expenditure on education had taken place in the late 20's increasing to over a million dollars in 1931. Drastic cuts took place in the depression which reduced this by half. The Commisssion early decided to spend what they could on education and by 1936-37 the public money expended was over the 1931 figure. When the wartime prosperity brought ample funds to the exchequer bold reconstruction schemes were put in hand. These consisted in the main of rebuilding or enlarging schools, particularly in the outports. In 1942 it was felt possible to abolish fees and make education, at least nominally, compulsory between the ages of 7-14. This reconstruction program was financed on a dollar for dollar basis. The local church personally responsible raised half the cost of reconstruction and the other half came from government funds. This reconstruction scheme gathered momentum and in three years, 1944-47, 211 new schools were built and 115 were rebuilt or enlarged; 32 per cent of the whole school population attended the schools affected. The Commission Government definitely took the view that whilst times were good education arrears should be made up. They had intended to spend at the rate of over half a million dollars a year until 1951, when they hoped that all schools would have been fitted with modern equipment, flush W.C.'s and proper heating. In the autumn of 1948, however, they decided to cut the annual expenditure on rebuilding schools by half in view of the uncertainty created by the approaching Confederation. There is no doubt, however, of the enormous work done in the past few years. In travelling round the country the impression is certainly created that every settlement has its new school.

Each of the three main religious organizations had created denominational colleges in St. John's for higher education. In theory these served the whole island but, in fact, only a limited number of children come as boarders to them from the outports. No less than 751 schools in 1948 out of a total of over 1,200 provided some form of secondary work in addition to elementary education; 173 of the 819 one-room schools were in this number. It can thus be said that whilst the Commission Government's help has very greatly improved elementary education in the island, secondary education has not benefited to the same extent from recent expansion and is still mainly fee paying in character. Plans have been drawn up to create a number of regional boarding schools which would take children of 13-17 in more advanced education, possibly with an agricultural bias. Certainly some such schools are essential if secondary education of an adequate character is to be made available to a widely scattered child population. Being boarding schools they could either be established by the different denominations or on a common school basis and could take pupils from a fairly wide area. The Department of Education envisages building a dozen such schools over the next ten years. A scheme to create a Catholic regional school on these lines to serve the southern part of the Avalon Peninsula has been actively discussed but has not yet come into being.

The University Memorial College in St. John's was created in 1925 very largely as a war memorial for the 1914-18 war although it has always received some government assistance. The course has been a two-year one and students have been expected to go on to other universities overseas to complete their degrees. It cannot be said that the system has worked out altogether satisfactorily although the teaching at the college has a high reputation and many former students hold good posts both in Government service and in local business concerns.

When the college was set up the three denominational secondary schools in St. John's were persuaded to hand over their last-year pupils to the college which thus started with 16-17-year-olds. This has robbed the secondary schools of their " prefect " class whilst making the age of Memorial College students very young. In fact a very large part of the students have only completed one year and only a small proportion have gone on to overseas universities. Of these a very large proportion have not returned to Newfoundland as it has not seemed to provide them with openings. Those who did come back of course had the advantage of the wider experience they had gained abroad. A certain number of scholarships have been given but the majority of students had to come up either on their own or their parents' resources. Able boys and girls from the outports have frequently had the expense and difficulty of obtaining lodgings although denominational schools have provided outport students with hostel accommodation. In recent years student teachers have become full members of the college and have certainly gained by mixing with other students.

The case for raising the status of the University College to that of a fully-fledged university is overwhelming. Faculties to meet all the needs of the students certainly could not be provided, at least, for many years to come. The development of the government service and of the major business houses in St. John's, as well as the needs of the paper companies should provide openings for a large number of the young men and women of the island. If the neighbouring Nova Scotia can make good use of four universities then Newfoundland should certainly be able to make good use of one.

A four-year course is general in North America and a new university would have to give its degrees on that basis. The first year could, with advantage, be taken at recognized secondary schools which could either be denominational colleges in St. John's, the proposed regional schools in the Provinces or some other secondary school which was recognized to be of a high standard. The restoration of these older pupils to the secondary schools would be a great boon to them and the curriculum for that year could definitely form a part of a university degree. Three years, that is one more than at present, could then be taken at the university. It would be necessary to adopt stricter standards for admittance if the big leakage, which at present takes place during the academic course, is to be checked. Not only would new lecture rooms be needed but a big expansion of hostel accommodation for the students. Fortunately there is plenty of room for expansion adjacent to the present Memorial College buildings. The proposed conversion of the Memorial College into a university is urgently required if those who are likely to hold responsible posts in Newfoundland and in the years ahead are to be adequately educated to carry out their jobs properly. It is surprising that the Commission Government did not support the proposal to raise funds for this development, in part at least, as a war memorial for the 1939-45 war. Funds for this purpose might well have come not only from former students and local businessmen but also from persons of Newfoundland origin in Canada and United States. A large part at least of the maintenance costs of the university, however, would have to come out of the island's exchequer. In its plans for the next ten years the Department of Education does not appear to have been definite as to whether it should or should not support this important development.

One of the most valuable courses which could certainly be taken at the proposed university would be something comparable to the Oxford Modern Greats, which could prepare students both for entering into the more important civil service posts as well as into the bigger business firms. Such a course would naturally have a number of alternative special subjects and a general Newfoundland bias, whilst placing the country and its problems against a world background. In addition there could be degrees in law and natural science. Some teacher trainees for secondary education work could take a degree although the majority of teacher trainees would probably prefer a shorter period of training. Those wishing to become doctors or agricultural specialists would probably still require to go overseas to complete their training for some years ahead. There should be nothing to prevent particular students also being sent overseas for further training in other fields if it was felt they would benefit from this.

Part of the large increase in expenditure on education has been due to a big rise in salaries. These are still low, however, compared with those of many other countries. The profession certainly recruits many of the ablest youngsters from the outports. In fact it is one of the few avenues by which persons of ability can acquire further education and a chance to rise in the world. In contrast to the U.S.A. teaching in Newfoundland enlists a considerable number of male entrants particularly to the Anglican, the United Church and common schools. Many of these, having secured their training and taught for a few years pass on to other jobs where their education stands them in good stead. The fact that many of the larger Catholic schools are staffed by members of religious orders discourages young Catholics from entering the profession; it is felt, therefore, that Catholics are at a certain disadvantage as they do not have the same opportunity of using the profession as a stepping stone to other jobs. The various increases in salaries of teachers, although felt to be far from adequate, have done something to curb too rapid a turnover in the profession. The creation of a powerful Teachers' Trade Union has enabled teachers not only to raise their grievances but also to take a more positive part in the running of summer schools, refresher courses, etc.

The Commission Government, in the middle 30's, overhauled the curriculum in the schools and brought it much more into line with Newfoundland needs. Better school books were produced and were supplied to pupils for a nominal fee, thus becoming their property. The net effect of the Commission Government's policy has been to provide Newfoundland with a system of elementary education which is better than in many of the rural parts of the other Canadian Provinces. There are still a few very small settlements without schools. Compulsory schooling is being enforced more strictly year by year and exceptions are only allowed now when a suitable school is not within travelling distance. The urgent need now is to improve secondary education by building at least some regional boarding schools and by enlarging the Memorial College into a full university.

The central administration of the Department of Education includes representatives of the four major denominations possessing schools—Anglican, Catholic, United Church and Salvation Army—together with a secretary. Despite the partial growth of the common school, denominationalism remains deeply rooted in the country. Not only does it reflect the strong religious feelings possessed by the majority of Newfoundlanders but, from the central Government's point of view, it has the advantage of raising a large part of the capital expenditure required for building and enlarging schools from local sources. This can be raised by the churches when it would be very difficult to raise anything like similar sums of money by some kind of local rate or taxation. Being itself part of the national tradition, denominationalism has been worked into a comprehensive national educational system. It can certainly be said that it will remain part of that system for a very long time ahead even though there may be some considerable expansion of the common school system in some of the larger and newer settlements. It would be foolish for anyone to try and interfere with this denominational system, as any such action would certainly hold up the large schemes for secondary schools and university development which the country still needs if its educational system is to be on effective modern lines.

Efforts have been made to develop visual aid in education and a film library of over 1,000 films has been created which travels around the country. Broadcasting has also been used to assist in the work of education not only in Newfoundland but also in Labrador, where the Moravian Mission is to create a small station at Nain in the near future.

There has been some development of adult education in Newfoundland, particularly since the advent of the Commission Government. This has been organized on lines similar to that of the Workers' Education Association in Great Britain. In addition to academic work considerable efforts have been made to develop the teaching of handicrafts, singing, dramatics, etc. There are over 1,000 adult education students in St. John's, and the movement is served throughout the country by 13 itinerant teachers.

A public library system was started in 1936 with the opening of the Gosling Memorial Library at St. John's, which was the first free library in the country. With some small financial assistance from the Carnegie Trust regional libraries have been created in all parts of the island. Twenty-six of these are now in existence and subsidies have been given in recent years to assist the construction of local libraries, which have been built frequently as war memorials. These regional libraries act as distributing centres for books and also receive subsidies from government funds to assist their operation. A Public Library Board, which includes the President of the Memorial University College, supervises this system which has grown very rapidly in the past few years. There is a large demand in the outports for easy fiction in addition to books concerned with various phases of Newfoundland life. The Board supplies lists of suitable books to the regional libraries. The Gosling Library is building up a collection of Newfoundland records and has taken over those which previously belonged to the House of Assembly. If the necessary funds were available the library service could expand very rapidly indeed, so great is the public demand.

Housing conditions in Newfoundland as a whole are good, especially in the outports. Wood is the normal material for construction and most Newfoundlanders have some knowledge of carpentry. Timber has been plentiful in the past and opportunities have existed in the autumn, at the end of the fishing season, to do building work. As families grew so houses could have extra storeys and rooms added. The habit of painting these wooden houses in bright colours makes the outport look very attractive when the houses, with neat white palings round the gardens, are in good condition. So long as settlements remain small and timber plentiful there is little danger of nuisances arising as a result of inadequate sanitation and overcrowding. Long-established fishing settlements, such as Brigus and others on the shores of Conception Bay and Curling and Bonne Bay on the west coast, are good examples of such settlements, which have grown up gradually and in which the owners have taken pride in building and maintaining decent homes. There must always, however, have been many settlements whose inhabitants had little to spare and whose homes were frequently unpainted shacks consisting of bits of wood just nailed together. As soon as a certain amount of prosperity came to a fishing community it showed itself in the building of new and better homes. I was told this had happened in the past few years at the settlement of Lourdes on the Port-au-Port Peninsula since the establishment of a co-operative among the local fishermen had brought them greater returns. I was approached, when there, by some of of the families, who had been transferred by the Commission from the south coast in the late 30's, to know when their owner-ship of their plots of land could be confirmed so that they could enlarge the small houses which had been given them at the time of their transference. The exhaustion of building timber in many parts of the island, however, has greatly increased building costs. The Government has wisely reserved some standing timber near the new settlement of Cormack for future development. It is highly desirable that other suitable stands should be kept for future use on the Port-au-Port Peninsula and wherever else they still survive in the coastal areas and near inland settlements.

In contrast to the outports are the larger towns where hous-ing standards are frequently bad, largely owing to lack of local government in the past and the services which it normally provides. At St. John's houses were built close upon one another as soon as the settlement became of any size. A number of devastating fires swept the town, the latest being in 1892. Most of the business houses have built their offices and ware-houses along Water Street in brick. The dwellings of the majority of the town's inhabitants were rebuilt in wood in rows climbing up the steep hills on the north side of the harbour.

128

Pouch Cove (Avalon Peninsula)—Fishing rooms and drying stages

Lomond (Bonne Bay)
— M o d e r n fishing
wharf and plant

St. John's—Ships in the harbour

Photo: Fox.

Today they are frequently dirty and decayed, being now close on sixty years old. Much of the centre of the island's capital city gives the unfortunate impression of being a piece of 19th century Liverpool the wrong side of the Atlantic. A Committee of Inquiry was set up on the St. John's housing problem in 1940. It pointed out the bad condition of many of the streets and the fact that many houses were connected with neither water supply nor sewers; their structure was, in many cases, so bad that this was not practicable. In all it was estimated there were 1,500 more families in St. John's than houses.

The Committee recommended the public purchase of a large area of land lying across the slope to the north of the town. This was to be developed by a special body, the St. John's Housing Corporation, which was to own the land, build houses and supply the necessary drains and other services. The city, which had hitherto been developing as a long narrow strip up the Waterford Valley, would be made a better shape as the new areas would lie fairly close to the centre of the town.

Starting in 1942 the housing corporation first laid out the site as a whole by putting in a main drain and new roads. Eight hundred and fifty acres of land in all were brought into public ownership and have since been included inside the city boundary. By the end of 1948 147 houses and 92 flats had been completed and the program in hand provided for 93 further dwellings. The cost of building proved to be a great deal higher than prewar despite the fact that the corporation made up many of the materials they required on the spot. It had been hoped that the better-off sections of the population would move into these new houses or flats which they could afford to pay for and thus free other accommodation for the poorer sections of the population. Following the end of the war, however, the corporation found it difficult to dispose of the houses they were building although the demand for flats proved far greater than had originally been expected. With the uncertainty of approaching Confederation, the corporation slowed down many of its activities. About half of the houses originally estimated to be required, if all families were to have homes of their own, have been built since 1942 in St. John's. Half of these have been put up privately, mainly in the direction of Waterford, although the corporation allowed private building on its land provided the houses fitted into the scheme of architectural development. The other half of the houses have been constructed by the corporation and are good examples of the best modern style; the blocks of flats in particular incorporate all the latest improvements.

The scheme, when completed, should have three main centres and should be landscaped with trees and open spaces. It seems likely that the new Provincial Government will complete the houses already under construction and landscape the area which will probably then be made over to the St. John's Municipal Council to administer and to complete at their leisure.

It should be pointed out, however, that this scheme, admirable though it is from a town planning point of view, makes no contribution towards the demolition of the slums of St. John's. If this is to be done a great deal more public money would have to be sunk to re-house the many families whose homes are in too bad a condition to make really habitable. How funds are to be found for this purpose is one of the problems which a poor country like Newfoundland is up against. In the meantime the city council has done a good deal to improve road surfaces and to include all the houses possible in the water and sewerage systems.

Outside St. John's the principal housing problems are in the new shack towns that have grown up not only around the paper towns but in places such as Deerlake, Botwood and Bishop's Falls. The introduction of local government at a place such as Corner Brook West has led to the insistence on concrete foundations for new houses and other elementary standards. Once local government has got well established in these areas it should be possible to insist on a gradual rebuilding of homes provided the earnings of their owners remain at a decent level. In view of the likely prosperity of the paper towns for some time to come, this should be possible. The early incorporation of any area likely to be developed would also help to prevent bad housing conditions arising. A small section of Bell Isle near the iron mines and other mining settlements like St. Lawrence also contain some bad housing; this is more difficult to deal with owing to the uncertain future of the mining industries.

All of these settlements have the big advantage over St. John's that the houses are usually detached standing on separate plots of land. There is, therefore, the possibility of reconstruction on the site and the planting of trees, gardens, etc., to create a pleasant community. An old town like Harbour Grace, whose population has greatly declined in the last half century, was faced with the problem of deserted houses whose owners had disappeared. Powers were given to the new local council to take over such property and a recent fire has enabled much of the town to be rebuilt.

Outside St. John's, where further special measures will have to be taken to deal with the slum problem, it should prove possible to get a big improvement in housing conditions when local government becomes a live force, provided that the country's industries remain in a fairly prosperous condition. Powers will probably have to be given to local councils, or to magistrates where they do not exist, to compel the pulling down and rebuilding of unsuitable houses when their owners can afford to rebuild them decently. Assistance might be given both by making building materials more easily available and putting at the disposal of builders a number of suitable plans of wooden houses in a number of different designs. From the point of view of creating decent communities to live in—and incidentally helping the tourist trade—it is to be hoped that these will be mainly on traditional local lines. The Mansard roof has been widely used in Newfoundland in the past and is suited to local conditions as are the Georgian types of windows which offer strong resistance to the wintry blast and are easy to repair if one of the panes breaks. A campaign of re-painting the whole of the outside of a house, perferably in traditional bright colours, every third year should certainly be pressed in government propaganda. Not only does this make a township cheerful but the paint keeps the house in good condition.

14

HEALTH AND OTHER SOCIAL SERVICES

It was long believed that most Newfoundlanders were tough and healthy specimens of humanity because of the hard life they led in the open air. The rapid increase in the population lent support to this view. It was not until Grenfell and other doctors began to make detailed studies of health conditions in some of the outports of northern Newfoundland and Labrador that some suspicion began to arise as to the extent of the bad health which afflicted so large a part of the population. As the present century advanced more and more information came to light about the unsatisfactory nutrition in the island. As early as 1912 Little had stated of Newfoundland that " a great many people here live from hand to mouth being always on the verge of poverty, and there are many who are satisfied if they have enough flour, tea and molasses to see them through the winter." He found a strong prejudice against wholemeal flour. For a large part of the year white bread, in conjunction with salt fish, beef and pork and margarine formed the main diet. Fresh meat or fish, vegetables and milk were consumed in limited quantities in many outports and then for only short periods of the year. Reports showed the universal prevalence of " bad stomach " due to frequent nutritional disorders; the physique of the children was often poor. They were usually up to normal height but under-weight and there was an absence of high spirits amounting almost to apathy.

From 1931 onwards medical survey after survey confirmed the widespread ill-effects of malnutrition upon the health of the people. True, the birth rate remained high but, as the following table for the year 1940 shows, Newfoundland's position was worse than all the countries named in infant mortality, maternity death rate, T.B. death rate and the general death rate:—

Country	Birth Rate	Infant Mortality	Maternity Death Rate	T.B. Death Rate	General Death Rate
Newfoundland	26.3	91.0	4.2	172.0	11.8
New Zealand	22.6	31.0	2.9	40.0	10.5
South Africa	25.3	52.0	2.5	34.0	9.6
Denmark	21.3	45.0	3.9	47.0	9.6
Norway	16.3	27.0	2.8	98.0	10.4
U.S.A.	21.9	40.0	3.8	46.0	10.9
Gt. Britain	17.2	54.0	3.2	64.0	12.1
Australia	17.9	36.0	3.6	39.0	10.3
Canada	21.5	21.4	4.0	51.0	9.7

Special studies of tuberculosis, the worst of Newfoundland's scourges, have shown that its incidence has dropped with the improvement in nutrition and standard of life of the population. Being a communicable disease, the overcrowded conditions, especially for sleeping, in many of the houses gave it an opportunity to develop which malnutrition has enhanced. As a result of these various inquiries it was decided to fortify the flour and margarine to make good some of their nutritional deficiencies. Then a Nutrition Council was set up in 1945 to advise the Government. During the large scale unemployment in the 30's the Commission Government decided to issue wholemeal flour as a form of relief. This certainly decreased the amount of beriberi in the island which increased once more, however, when improved conditions of employment led to the resumption of the eating of white bread after 1940. Unfortunately a strong dislike of brown flour was created which tended to be identified in the public mind with relief. The greater difficulty of keeping this flour had given some real basis for the prejudice and made it impracticable for the Government to increase the extraction rate of the flour when they decided to fortify it. The low consumption of milk, either fresh, tinned or dry, made it necessary to add calcium to the flour if an attempt was to be made to give Newfoundlanders better bones and teeth in future.

A report made by Doctor Cuthbertson on nutrition in Newfoundland, as a result of a visit he paid in the summer of 1945, showed that the fortification of the flour and marga-rine had produced some considerable improvements in health. He recommended the adoption of Canada approved flour (with a 78 per cent extraction rate) plus some revision in the

fortifying which, he believed, would lead to further improvements. The Nutrition Council appears to have kept a watch
on the position to date but the Government have been
frightened about carrying out all Doctor Cuthbertson's suggestions for fear that they could not carry public opinion with
them.

Much has been done to educate the population, particularly
the housewives, to increase their production and consumption
of milk, fresh vegetables and fruit and to make more use of
cod liver oil and of fatty fish such as herring. The Agricultural Department combined with that of Health and Social
Welfare to try and persuade the inhabitants of the outports to
produce such articles of food. The tariff was removed on fresh
fruit and fruit juices, but the cost of fruit distribution, with its
many and long distances, remained high. Suggestions for
widening consumption by school children of milk, cocoa, milk
powder or milk chocolate have made little progress owing to
the high cost of milk production in the island and the heavy
budgetry expenditure which would be involved in giving any
of these products free to all school children.

A general improvement in nutrition has taken place with
better employment conditions since 1940 and has already had
a considerable effect on the country's health. A long-term
policy of government assistance combined with education will
be necessary before the nutritional problem is solved in Newfoundland. More use might perhaps be made of the radio as
well as Nonia and the various Women's Welfare Organizations
in teaching the population how to obtain and cook a good diet
whilst teachers, teacher trainees and clergy, who are likely to
have a big educational influence, should be taught to give a
lead in the matter. Something might also be done by the paper
and mining companies to improve the nutritional standard of
the food served in their canteens.

In addition to using the schools to educate future generations in the use of a better diet, the Government could also use
them to introduce a more suitable clothing for children in the
summer months. Parents naturally clothe them as fully as
possible to guard against the cold of winter and spring. In a
land with a comparative short summer there is much to be said
for Grenfell's proposals that both boys and girls should do
without stockings and schoolboys wear open-necked shirts and

shorts as a school uniform during that period so as to get the maximum benefit from sun and fresh air. Such a change would not only be healthier but cheaper from the point of view of the parents as reducing wear—and tear—on superfluous clothes for a few months.

At the advent of Commission Government in 1934 there were few hospital facilities outside St. John's and those in the capital were far from adequate. Grenfell had opened his hospital at St. Anthony in the Petty Nord and had established a medical service along the Labrador coast to give such service as it could to the summer fishermen from Newfoundland and to the local liviers. The Grenfell Association had come into being to provide this service largely with funds at first from Britain and then increasingly from the United States. The paper companies had also provided some services in the paper towns and for their loggers. A program was put in hand for expanding hospital services in the capital and for building up a service of cottage hospitals around the coasts in the most suitably situated outports. During the war the occupying forces, particularly the Canadians, constructed hospital facilities in St. John's as well as at Gander and Botwood. By agreement these were passed over to the Newfoundland Government at the end of the war. A large part of the extra revenue coming in to the Exchequer during and after the war was utilized for extending existing hospital accommodation and for fitting up these new ones. Plans were also put in hand for constructing and opening large sanatoria on the west coast at Corner Brook and St. John's, for T.B. patients. Both the mental hospital and the home for the aged are grossly overcrowded and require extended premises at an early date. The completion of this program was held up during the negotiations on Confederation but it should be carried on in the near future.

Efforts have been made to work the Catholic hospitals in St. John's, the Notre Dame hospital at Twillingate and the Grenfell hospitals into a comprehensive national service. Some assistance has been given from public funds to these private hospitals and a large number of the doctors and dentists in the island receive much of their salaries from public funds. Contributions have been collected towards these services from the local population where a hospital or nursing station of some kind was available for their use. Some part of the cost of running the services is thus recovered although no payment is demanded from those who are badly off. The total cost of the considerable improvements in health services provided during the 40's has been very large indeed and the number of persons employed in staffing them has risen from 393 in 1936/7 to well over 1,000 at the end of 1948. There was still a very considerable deficiency in the numbers of doctors, dentists and nurses required. The Commission Government introduced a scheme for sending able young men and women overseas to secure medical training on condition that they promised to return for service in Newfoundland for a certain number of years. The difficulty of finding places for medical students after the war in universities both sides of the Atlantic seriously interfered with the scheme.

To deal with the low standard of life and its effects on the physique and morale of the population, the Government attempted to build up a number of social services. In the middle of the 19th century considerable sums had to be given in relief by the Government when conditions in the fisheries were bad, and at some periods, the sums of money paid out amounted to a very large part of the national expenditure although the relief paid to the individual and his family was small. In normal years it was expected that the merchant would help to carry the fishermen through the winter. This unfortunate dependence on the merchant prevented the fishermen from building up any reserves to fall back on when bad times came. The Government's encouragement of railway construction in the last two decades of the 19th century owed a good deal to a desire to provide employment for Newfoundlanders in preference to giving relief. Later road construction was pushed ahead, frequently in a very piecemeal manner, as a constructive alternative to relief. All circles in Newfoundland welcomed the drop in the total paid out for relief when the construction of the American bases began the wartime boom. Increases were made in the amount of relief payments with the rise in the cost of living. The Commission Government, however, much preferred to go ahead with development schemes which would be of lasting value to the people and was unwilling to increase relief payments in case the country should be saddled with scales it could not afford to maintain from its own revenues should a slump come after the war. As a result of the special inquiry conducted by Doctors Garland and D'Arcy Hart into the incidence of T.B. in the island (1945) a large increase was made in relief payments due to their belief that this would reduce the danger from T.B. by improving living standards and the natural resistance to the disease. The amount paid out in relief has always varied enormously from month to month, being particularly high early in the New Year.

A very limited scheme had been created in Newfoundland for old age pensions. At the date of Confederation these were not available until a man had passed the age of 75 and were quite inadequate to maintain the aged in comfort. Payments for the casual sick and widows and orphans were also extraordinarily low. It was the realization that the country was not rich enough by itself to provide anything like the standard of social services which were generally recognized to be desirable everywhere among English-speaking peoples which played a large part in the agitation over Confederation. The terms of union with Canada provided that Canada would " extend to the Province of Newfoundland, on the same basis and subject to the same terms and conditions as in the case of other Provinces of Canada, the welfare and other public services provided from time to time by Canada for the people of Canada generally." It was made clear that this would include unemployment insurance benefits, merchant seamen benefits, family allowances, old age and blind pensions and assistance for housing. Much support was secured also for Confederation in the outports owing to the belief that the removal or reduction of the high Newfoundland tariff would cheapen the cost of living for the worst-off sections of the people.

A Division of Child Welfare, which took over all the social welfare problems connected with children from various other government departments, was first set up in November, 1943. This division, which is now operated under the Welfare of Children Act, 1944, has sought to enforce school attendance in St. John's since that became compulsory, has supervised the juvenile courts and probation services and has looked after neglected children and children for adoption. A special boys' home was opened for serious delinquents under 18, first at Whitbourne and then, after a fire had destroyed their school, in an old camp at Bell Isle. This has served as a useful boarding school for training and placing difficult youths. The department as a whole has certainly justified its creation in assisting some of the more difficult elements among Newfoundland's large child population.

Veterans' affairs have also been looked after by the Department of Health and Welfare both through the administration of pensions and the organization of resettlement schemes. The Act of Union made available to Newfoundland veterans the more numerous benefits which had been made avaible to Canadian veterans. The Newfoundland Government, following demobilization both of men from the Armed Forces and from the Forestry Corps, provided a wide variety of training facilities extending from support at the Memorial College or attendance at overseas universities to vocational training in Newfoundland or, in special cases, in Canada, United States or Great Britain, for particular trades. Special assistance was given to those wishing to settle on the land, to obtain fishing outfits or to open small industries. The Ex-Servicemen's Vocational Training School in St. John's appears to have done a particularly good job in training men for re-establishment in civil life. The paper companies and the government services, such as Gander Airport, the railways and telecommunications, made special drives to obtain men who had acquired special training or experience whilst overseas.

15

THE LABRADOR

THE Labrador coast had been discovered by the Norsemen, the English and the Portuguese at the same time as they discovered Newfoundland. The latter gave it its name. Fishermen of all nations visited its coasts in the 16th and 17th centuries in the same way as they visited the coast of Newfoundland. About 1600 their headquarters was the settlement of Brest on the north shores of the straits of Belle Isle. Later the Labrador fisheries became limited to the French and English who came both from the home countries and from their North American settlements. As soon as the north-east coast of Newfoundland, between Twillingate and Bonavista was settled in the 18th century some of the fishermen from that area began to frequent the Labrador coast for the summer fishing. After the British conquest of French Canada, the Labrador coast as far as the river St. John's in the Gulf of St. Lawrence, was placed under the authority of the Governor of Newfoundland (1763). Friction arose at the interference which resulted with the traditional French-Canadian fisheries on the northern shores of the Gulf of St. Lawrence. In 1774 the whole of Labrador was, therefore, transferred to the Province of Quebec. Newfoundlanders now protested at discrimination against them, with the result that the coast was once more placed under the Governor of Newfoundland in 1809. Finally, in 1825, a compromise was reached by which the northern shore of the Gulf of St. Lawrence as far as Blanc Sablon was placed under Quebec whereas the Labrador coast on the straits of Belle Isle and the Atlantic as far north as Cape Chidley remained under Newfoundland.

This compromise worked satisfactorily until questions about development of the interior began to come up. A dispute then arose as to whether Newfoundland's authority in Labrador was restricted just to the coast line between Blanc Sablon and Cape Chidley or whether it covered the whole hinterland of the coast inland as far as the " height of land." The issue was finally referred to the British Privy Council for arbitration which, in 1927, granted practically all the Newfoundland claim. As a result, therefore, Newfoundland was confirmed in possession of 120,000 square miles of territory including the whole basin of the Hamilton River.

As has been described elsewhere the coast between Blanc Sablon and Hamilton Inlet has been gradually settled by Newfoundlanders. In the late 19th century the fishery off " the Labrador " was at the height of its prosperity. In 1891 it is recorded that 1,861 vessels took part in the fishery containing 10,478 men, 2,087 women and 828 children. The greater part of these came from Newfoundland for the summer and returned home in the fall although a small number stayed the year through on the Labrador coast. In addition, a considerable number of vessels from New England, Nova Scotia and even Great Britain took part in the fishery. In the last 60 years this salt cod fishery has greatly declined in importance and is now entirely limited to Newfoundlanders and liviers on the Labrador coast.

The Grenfell Association, which originally started as a mission to the fishermen, has now established hospitals and schools at suitable points at the head of inlets where it can serve the permanent inhabitants right through the year as well as assist the yearly visitors on the coast. The very valuable work it has done has been paralleled by that of the Moravian Mission to the Eskimos and halfbreeds on the northern part of the coast above the Hamilton Inlet. There is little doubt that but for the work of the Moravian Mission the Eskimos would have disappeared from this coast. As it was serious ravages of disease, and in particular the influenza epidemic of 1918, very seriously reduced their numbers although the total of Eskimos and halfbreeds is now approaching 1,000 once more. The Grenfell Mission encouraged the establishment of small co-operative stores in southern Labrador as in northern Newfoundland. The Moravians themselves established stores to purchase goods from the Eskimos and sell them what they wanted in the way of European supplies. Not making a financial success of their stores they handed them over to the Hudson Bay Company which already possessed a number of other stores in Labrador. Unfortunately, the company's desire for skins led the Eskimos to overhunt the coast and to neglect the catching of fish. In 1942 the Hudson Bay Company suddenly decided to give up all its posts in Newfoundland and Labrador save that at Northwest River. The Commission Government took over these posts in northern Labrador to save the situation. These stores have since been successfully run by the Department of Natural Resources who have sold $150,000 worth of cod fish, seals, furs, pickled sea trout, etc., yearly. Food supplies have been laid up at the stores to last through the spring as well as the winter so as to avoid the previous periods of semi-starvation before the new supplies came in. By encouraging the Eskimos to take part in all their traditional activities their diet —and physique—have been much improved.

The Labrador Indians, in the main, travel down to ports on the Gulf of St. Lawrence though some of them frequent Northwest River. Recently attempts have been made to establish at Okkak Bay a Roman Catholic Mission for the neglected Nascopi Indians who spend most of their time in the interior of Ungava.

The boundary dispute delayed exploitation of the forests along the Hamilton River. Northwest River on Hamilton Inlet developed as a successful trapping centre once the Grenfell Association had opened their school and hospital there. The construction of the Canadian airport at Goose and of the loggers' settlement at Port Hope Simpson have led to some increase in Labrador's population but in 1948 it was still estimated at only 5,718. The proposed iron mines in the upper Hamilton River Valley, a possible paper mill at Goose and some enlargement of the staff at the airport there should all lead to further substantial growth in population in the next few decades. So far, however, apart from the fisheries on the coast, little has been done to develop the timber, mineral, water power and other sources of the country. A mapping of this immense territory from the air is in progress but it will be a long time before a thorough geological survey can be carried out over the whole of this vast territory.

From time to time during the difficult period before the Commission Government took over, proposals were put forward for selling Labrador to Canada. Legends have grown up in Newfoundland about the potential wealth of the Labrador dependency. Very little, however, was done either to find out or develop its resources. Confederation should assist the mapping and surveying of this land which, despite its barrenness offers an outlet for Newfoundland's increasing population. There is little scope for the growing of vegtables or keeping of live-stock save round Hamilton Inlet and at the head of some of the more sheltered bays. Owing to the difficulty and expense of importing foodstuffs it is desirable that such pockets of shel-tered land as there are should be made the best use of and that the greenhouses introduced by the Moravian Mission, to give an early start to vegetables, should be established in every settlement. The possibility of introducing reindeer herds and fur farms also needs consideration.

During the long period that the Labrador coast was depen-dent upon Newfoundland, little was done to introduce any kind of regular administration before the advent of the Com-mission Government (1934). During this period Labrador did not even have representation in the Newfoundland House of Assembly. Under the Commission, Rangers were established in the most important settlements as agents of the Newfound-land Government and " the Labrador " made into a magis-trate's district. The school, hospitals and other services of the Grenfell and Moravian Missions were worked into the New-foundland educational and health services and the Department of Natural Resources made some efforts to get the country's natural resources investigated and developed. A Member was granted to Labrador in the National Convention and it is to be represented in future Houses of Assembly. In the past the Hudson Bay Company, the Grenfell Association and the Moravian Mission recruited their officials in the main from Scot-land, England and Germany. An important result of this new interest has been the filling of the growing number of govern-ment posts in the country largely by Newfoundlanders, as well as the sending of an increasing number of the local boys and girls for further education in Newfoundland. I was told in 1948 that an able Eskimo boy was then in training to become a doctor and return to serve his people. Newfoundland will certainly see that future developments in the country are staffed as far as possible by its own inhabitants or Newfoundlanders. The assimilation of Labrador to Newfoundland is thus likely to increase with its development.

There is need for Newfoundland to keep watch on the town

planning of the new iron ore towns to see that the country's resources are not only fully investigated and developed but that the necessary social services are provided for all its inhabitants. A proposal to set up a special department for Labrador under the Commissioner of Natural Resources unfortunately failed during the Commission Government. There is a strong case for creating a special Department of Labrador with a responsible Minister in the Provincial Government to supervise and push developments in this vast territory. Distances are so great that it is difficult for local officials to keep in touch with their relevant departments in St. John's. Relations with Quebec are bound to grow as the iron mines are opened up. A special department for Labrador could keep a watch on these. To help future administration some revision of the southern border of Newfoundland-Labrador, now a straight line on the map, might be made so as to transfer to Quebec the headwaters of the rivers running into the Gulf of St. Lawrence; the border would then run the whole way from Blanc Sablon to Cape Chidley along the " height of land."

16

CONFEDERATION AND AFTER

CONFEDERATION came into operation on April 1, 1949. The Canadian Cabinet took into its ranks Bradley, who had been chairman of the Convention and Attorney General in one of the Governments before 1934, he was to act as a link with the new Province during the period of transition. Walsh, the first Lieutenant-Governor, asked J. R. Smallwood, the Confederate leader to form the first Provincial Government. He divided up the various departments which remained the responsibility of the Provincial Government among himself and eleven other Ministers. These were drawn from all parts of the island in an attempt to build up a national Government; two of their number were former Commissioners. This new Government was to hold office until a general election had taken place when it was to be replaced by one responsible to the newly elected House of Assembly. Elections had to be held within four months of the coming into operation of the Act of Union.

" Joey " Smallwood's views on political and economic questions were certainly progressive. This young man, who was still only 48 at the date of Confederation, had been actively associated with the Liberal Party under Responsible Government, but had not been identified with any particular political group during the days of the Commission. He had, however, taken an active part both in the co-operative and trade union movements and certainly favoured an extension of government initiative in developing the country's economic resources and its social services. He thus promised legislation to create a commission to regulate and control all public utilities such as hydro-electric power and to compel employers to negotiate with accredited unions. Further assistance was promised the co-operative movement. Realizing the value to Newfoundland of the terms of union which had been offered by the Canadian Federal Liberal Government and believing, as it proved rightly, that it would continue in office after the approaching general election, Smallwood and his friends naturally linked up with that party. This alliance was helped by the fact that, to meet the attack from the Canadian Socialists (C.C.F.), the Canadian Liberals had moved leftward in recent years especially in the field of the social services. Smallwood himself achieved an oratorical triumph when he visited the Canadian Liberal Convention which was pleased to receive the accession of strength which Smallwood was able to bring with him from Newfoundland. Some of his statements during the election campaign, however, proved somewhat embarrassing and it remains to be seen whether his mercurial personality can remain associated with the solid " middle of the road " Canadian Liberals. In the elections, both provincial and federal, the Liberals mainly stood on their record as the party which had secured Newfoundland all the advantages which came from Confederation. They had the great tactical advantage of having recently taken office; the payment of the second instalment of the " baby bonus " just before the provincial elections clinched their position. Once the decision had been taken many prominent opponents of Confederation, such as Chesley Crosbie, joined the Liberal ranks to help in the job of making Newfoundland a success in its new role as a Canadian Province.

The majority of the opponents of Confederation accepted the referenda decisions and formed a local Progressive Conservative party in association with the Canadian party of that name. In their election campaigns they pressed for a reopening of the terms of union to give Newfoundland better financial terms and claimed that they would be able to iron out dollar-sterling difficulties. Peter Cashin, the most diehard of the opponents of Confederation, carried on the fight to the bitter end even after most anti-Confederates had accepted the union as inevitable. An attempt by the Canadian Socialists (C.C.F.) to establish themselves in the Province met with little success.

The Provincial Election showed an overwhelming Liberal majority thus ratifying the refendum decision in favour of Confederation and confirming the Smallwood Government in power. The popular vote was well over two to one for the Liberals who had the largest majority ever secured in a Newfoundland election on a remarkably heavy poll. Not only did the victors emphatically win all the districts which had supported Confederation in 1948 but they invaded the Avalon Peninsula and took two of the four seats in St. John's and all those round Conception Bay save the two for the Bell Island-Harbour Main district. In all the Liberals won 22 seats, the Progressive Conservatives five while Peter Cashin, the resolute opponent of Confederation, was returned as an Independent. In the ensuing federal elections the Liberals carried off five of the seven seats in Newfoundland, failing only to win the two St. John's seats. A large number of the Conservative candidates outside the Avalon Peninsula in the provincial elections lost their deposits through failing to get a third of the votes cast for their opponents.

The Canadian Socialists (C.C.F.) are unlikely to get much support in the near future in Newfoundland if Smallwood actively attempts to fulfil the hopes of those who voted for his party. Should Smallwood's party disappoint the outport voters, particularly those of the west coast, a local branch of the C.C.F. would grow rapidly. The significance of the referenda votes and of the subsequent election returns was the revolt against the former leadership of the Water Street merchants. Those who voted with Smallwood wanted constructive economic and social developments; they are likely, therefore, to support parties both in federal and provincial elections who can offer them such a policy. Smallwood himself, if any serious friction arises in future with the Liberal federal leaders, might well be forced to link up with the C.C.F. His own policies might well take him in that direction. Should the tide turn once more and large scale electoral successes come to the C.C.F. in federal politics and in other provincial elections they could have a profound effect on the position in Newfoundland.

The amazing prosperity of the late war years has continued and the last year of the Commission Government showed not only a further surplus but the largest total volume of trade in the country's history with exports and imports between them amounting to over 200 million dollars. So long as such prosperity lasts the Government is likely to continue to extend its hospital and education services. The advantages of a planned economy seem fairly widely accepted in Newfoundland and the Government will do its best to encourage new economic developments so as to make use of the country's various natural resources. A possible slump in the future should not, however, be overlooked. Newfoundland's prosperity is still based on the fisheries and paper. The example of Saskatchewan, when its wheat markets disappeared in 1929, should not be forgotten. No Canadian Federal Government, however, is likely to allow a depression to develop without making some efforts to deal with it. If Newfoundland were to get into economic difficulties she would certainly look to the Canadian Federal Government for active assistance. If bad times do not come for some years she is likely to keep very much more to herself.

In the long run Newfoundland's contacts with the other Maritime Provinces are likely to be increased and the Act of Union will certainly increase the influence of the Atlantic Maritime Provinces in the federation as a whole. Newfoundland has already learnt much from the co-operative movement in Nova Scotia. Close co-operation is likely to develop between the fisheries of the whole Canadian Atlantic seaboard.

A very considerable amount of emigration has taken place from Newfoundland ever since the middle of the 19th century. It was estimated in 1941 that there were 21,361 Newfoundlanders in the United States and 25,837 in Canada. Out of a forestry corps of 3,000 men who came to Britain to work during 1939-1945, 408 were discharged in Great Britain. The union with Canada and American immigration restrictions are likely to encourage migration to other parts of the Dominion. Newfoundland's increasing population is likely to be large enough both to provide the necessary labour force for new developments within the Province in addition to continuing the stream up the St. Lawrence. There is nothing unhealthy in such a situation if the standard of life continues to rise and further development of resources takes place in the Province. Remittances from emigrants are—and are likely to continue to be—of advantage to the island.

It is to be hoped that the Canadian Federal Government will be able to look after the needs of Newfoundland in commercial negotiations with foreign countries, particularly with the United States. Confederates, during the referenda discussions, made much of the point that the larger country would be in a stronger position to get good terms for the entry of Newfoundland products into overseas markets and to see that the maximum possible use was made of Newfoundland's air facilities. If these arguments should prove to have been wrong, bitter resentment over Confederation might arise in the island. If conditions continue fairly favourable, then opposition to Confederation is likely to disappear rapidly save for that of a small disappointed vocal minority.

Union with Canada, with the increasing influx of American tourists hoped for, is bound to have a big influence on the way of life of Newfoundlanders. The British tradition has been strong and contacts by sea and air and through the paper industry are likely to remain important although less than during the period of Commission Government. Tea and rum remain the national drinks in Newfoundland and are unlikely to give place to the American coffee and whisky. Cricket and rugger are no longer played but the British soccer is one of the three national games along with the American baseball and Canadian ice hockey. If Newfoundland is to provide a full and rich life for its inhabitants it must build up a way of life and a tradition that is definitely Newfoundland in character and not an imitation of that of the United States, Ontario or England. The country must always be prepared to borrow what is best and suitable from the traditions of other English-speaking peoples but it must adapt them if necessary to the local background. Particular attention should also be paid to the achievements of other northern peoples, such as the Scandinavians, Icelanders and Finns whose climate, products, problems and countryside are similar to that of Newfoundland. For long it appeared that the Canadian Maritime Provinces would go into decay but in recent years efforts have been made to build up in Nova Scotia a society with a distinctive local character. This has already provided Newfoundland with many useful lessons. Being even more isolated than Nova Scotia, Newfoundland has an even greater need for reconciling her traditions and institutions to her own local background. If this can be done Newfoundland will have contributed a valuable unit to strengthen the Canadian Confederation and, at the same time, have strengthened her own distinctive individual character.

APPENDIX I

BIBLIOGRAPHY

W. E. CORMACK. A Journey across the island of New-
foundland in 1822   1873
D. W. PROWSE. History of Newfoundland   1895
J. P. ROGERS. Newfoundland, Vol. IV, Part IV.
Historical Geography of British Colonies   ...   1911
SIR WILFRED GRENFELL. The Story of a Labrador
Doctor   1932
H. F. GURNEY. Economic Conditions in Newfound-
land—Report by H.M. Trade Commissioner in
Newfoundland and Maritime Provinces   1933
AMULREE. Report of Newfoundland Royal Commission   1933
J. R. SMALLWOOD. " The Book of Newfoundland "
Vols. I and II   1937
R. B. EWBANK. Public Affairs in Newfoundland   ...   1939
THOS. LODGE. Dictatorship in Newfoundland   ...   1939
GERALD S. GRAHAM. Sea Power and British North
America (1783-1820)   1941
A. H. MCLINTOCK. The Establishment of Constitu-
tional Government in Newfoundland (1783-1832)   1941
AMMON. Newfoundland: The Forgotten Island—
Report by Lord Ammon   1944
V. TANNER. Newfoundland Labrador, Vols. I
and II   1944
H. L. KEENLEYSIDE. Place names of Newfoundland,
Can. Geog. Jour. XXIX (6)   1944
NEWFOUNDLAND INDUSTRIAL DEVELOPMENT BOARD.
Information Booklet of Newfoundland and
Labrador   1945
MEDICAL SURVEY. Report on Nutrition in Newfound-
land by eleven investigators   1945
T. O. GARLAND and P. D'ARCY HART. Report on
Tuberculosis in Newfoundland   1945

R. A. MACKAY. Newfoundland, Economic, Diplomatic and Strategic Studies 1946

REPORT TO DOMINIONS OFFICE. Financial and Economic Position of Newfoundland 1946

R. GUSHUE. Report of Fisheries Postwar Planning Committee, Newfoundland 1946

GRIFFITH TAYLOR. Newfoundland: A Study of Settlement 1946

D. P. CUTHBERTSON. Report on Nutrition in Newfoundland 1947

REPORTS OF AND FOR SUB-COMMITTEES OF THE NATIONAL CONVENTION 1946-1947

MICHAEL BROSNAN. Pioneer History of St. George's Diocese 1948

ACT OF UNION WITH CANADA 1949

B. V. GUTSELL. An Introduction to the Geography of Newfoundland 1949

NEWFOUNDLAND POPULATION—RECENT CHANGES

Districts	1935	1945	Percentage Increase or Decrease
NORTH-EAST COAST			
White Bay	8,721	10,745	
Green Bay	8,257	8,606	
Grand Falls	14,373	19,458	
Twillingate	8,798	9,566	
Fogo	9,590	10,077	
Bonavista North	12,319	12,978	
	62,058	71,430	15.01
EAST COAST—CONCEPTION BAY			
Bonavista South	11,753	11,584	
Trinity North	12,766	12,808	
Trinity South	11,088	10,983	
Carbonear—			
Bay-de-Verde	13,409	12,825	
Harbour Grace	7,563	7,249	
Port-de-Grave	8,750	8,278	
	65,329	63,727	−2.45
ST. JOHN'S—BELL ISLAND AREA			
St. John's West	29,565	36,435	
St. John's East	25,321	28,821	
Harbour Main—			
Bell Island	15,017	17,549	
	69,903	82,805	18.46

SOUTH COAST

Ferryland	6,682	6,346	
Placentia—St. Mary's	8,454	9,448	
Placentia West	9,575	9,653	
Burin	10,668	10,940	
Fortune—Hermitage	11,334	11,445	
Burgeo—La Poile	9,293	9,357	
	56,006	57,189	2.11

WEST COAST

St. George—Port-au-Port	9,748	13,074	
Humber	15,166	20,560	
St. Barbe	6,662	7,509	
	31,576	41,143	30.30

LABRADOR	4,716	5,525	17.15
Total	289,588	321,819	11.13

INDEX

Acadians, 11
Act of Union, 47, 57
Adult Education, 127
Agricultural Department, 94, 99, 102-3
Agricultural Marketing, 101-4
Alcock and Brown, 85, 116
American Bases, 28, 88, 103, 108, 136
American Fishery Claims, 14, 23
American-Canadian trade relations, 55
American Market, 31, 52, 53
American Smelting and Refining Co., 68
Amulree Report, 36
Anglicans, 15, 16, 33, 120, 125-6
Anglo-Newfoundland Development Co., 45, 59-62, 68, 102
Antigonish, 105
Argentia, 88
Argentine, 61
Attlee, C. R., 40
Avalon Peninsula, 12-17, 24, 31-33, 60-72, 82-84, 90-99, 103, 114-123, 146
Avalon Telephone Co., 89
Aviation, 85-88

Baby Bonuses, 31
Badger, 83
Bait Issue, 23
Bell Isle, 10, 14, 37, 47, 68, 70, 110, 146
Bennett, 23
Bishop's Falls, 42, 60, 84
Boethics, 11
Bonavista, 18, 24, 37, 42, 47, 64, 78, 83, 89, 151
Bond, 26
Bonne Bay, 37, 128
Botwood, 42, 60, 61, 70, 79, 87, 113, 116, 135

Bowater's, 44, 45, 59, 60, 62, 66, 67, 70, 96, 97, 102
Bradley, 144
Brigus, 128
Bristol, 12, 17
Britain, 12-25, 30, 56-70, 135-148
Buchans, 10, 25, 39, 68-70, 81-87, 106, 116
Burin, 10, 70, 83, 152

Cabinet, 35, 47-48, 144
Cables, 89
Cabot, 11
Cabot way, 83
Canada, 9-16, 22-36, 62-93, 99-124, 138-148
Canadian Bases, 28, 108
Canadian Broadcasting Corporation, 91
Canadian National Railways, 81-82, 85
Canning, 56-57, 77-78
Cape Breton, 32
Carbonear, 37, 83, 151
Cartyville, 102-103
Cashin, Peter, 145-146
Catholics, 15-18, 31, 120-126, 135, 141
Central Government, 35-37, 47-48
Channel, 37
Channel Islands, 11-16
Child Welfare, 137-8
Civil Service, 36-37, 109
Clarenville, 37, 57, 65, 76-78, 85
Coaker, 24
Cochrane, 21
Codroy Valley, 78-84, 92-98, 102, 105
Commission Government, 27-36, 40-42, 47-51, 68-86, 94-99, 105-112, 121-146

153

Common Schools, 121
Company Towns, 39, 42-45
Confederation, 23-24, 30-41, 55,
  66, 71, 81, 90, 110, 129-148
Conception Bay, 12, 14, 18, 47,
  76, 79, 82, 92, 99, 128, 146
Convention, 29-30, 86, 110, 122,
  144
Co-operatives, 56, 102-108, 140
Co-operative Department, 35,
  48, 106
C.C.F., 145-146
Cormack, 18, 62, 83-84, 95-100,
  103, 105, 121, 128
Corner Brook, 17, 37, 44-45, 60,
  67, 74-83, 89-97, 100-103,
  113-121
Corner Brook East, 44
Corner Brook West, 40, 44
Crosbie, Chesley, 31, 145
Cupids, 12
Curling, 18, 44-45, 128
Cuthbertson, Dr., 133-134

Daily Mail, 60
Deer Lake, 42, 60, 70, 81-83,
  103
Denominational Colleges, 122-
  123
Denominationalism, 126
Devon, 11
Dialects, 17-18
Distribution Costs, 79
Dominion Steel and Coal Co.,
  68-70
Dorset, 11, 17
Drink Laws, 117
Dunn, P. D. H., 7, 27, 52-53,
  78, 96

Education Department, 48, 120-
  127
Elementary Education, 120-122,
  127
Emigration—from Newfound-
  land, 13, 16, 147
Englee, 53
English, 10-23, 45

Eskimos, 11, 15-19, 101, 140-
  142
Exploits River, 10, 59-60, 72,
  80-83

Ferryland, 12, 152
Finance Department, 35, 48
Finland, 65
Fire fighting, 64
Fisheries Board, 7, 51-58
Fisheries Department, 48, 51
Fishermen's Protective Union,
  24, 39, 109
Fishery Products Co., 53
Fluorspar mining, 10, 70
Forest Insect Survey, 64
Forestry, 59-66
Forestry Department, 63-65
France, 11-23
French Fishery Claims, 11-23
Frozen Fish Trade, 50-55
Fur Ranching, 101
Furness Withy and Co., 85

Gaelic, 17
Game Laws, 113
Gambo, 17, 59
Gander, 7, 10, 18, 43-44, 59-61,
  81-94, 103, 116, 121, 135-142
Geological Survey, 68
Germany, 68
Gilbert, 12
Goose, 12, 15, 37, 43, 66, 72,
  87-88, 141
Gosling Library, 127
Grand Bank, 37
Grand Falls, 37, 40, 45, 60, 66,
  76-94, 102-105, 114, 151
Gray River, 72
Grenfell, 100, 132-135
Grenfell Association, 8, 105,
  120-121, 135
Gros Morne, 10
Gushue, 7, 51, 57

Halifax, 85
Hall's Bay, 59, 80-83, 93
Hamilton, 21
Hamilton Falls, 10, 73

Hamilton Inlet, 15, 59, 66, 71-73, 101, 140-142
Hamilton River, 10, 59, 66, 71-73
Hampden, 18, 61
Happy Valley, 43
Harbour Breton, 37
Harbour Grace, 14, 18, 37, 80, 151
Harbour Main, 37, 146, 151
Harmons Field, 88
Health and Welfare Department, 42, 48
Heatherton, 103
Herring Fisheries, 50, 55
Home Affairs Department, 36
Hope Simpson, 27, 38
Hospital Conditions, 135-136
Hotels, 116
House of Assembly, 21-29, 41-48, 82, 142
Housing—Outports, 127-128
—St. John's, 128-130
—Shack towns, 39, 130-131
Hudson Bay, 35, 140-141
Humber Valley, 10, 59-61, 72, 84, 92-96, 102, 110, 152
Hydro-electric Resources, 72-73

Iceland, 11, 148
Imperial Tobacco Co., 76
Indians, 11, 17, 141
Indian Brook, 59, 83, 93
Ireland, 9-11, 17-23, 33
Iron Ore Mining, 68-72, 141-142

Jackatars, 11, 17
Jehovah's Witnesses, 16
Jews, 11
Job Bros., 52
Justice Department, 36, 48

Labour Department, 48, 110
Labour Problems, 107-108
Labour Relations Officer, 36
Labourers' Union, 109
Labrador, 9-10, 14-22, 29-37, 43-50, 55-59, 66-82, 88-90, 101, 120, 132, 139-143, 152

Labrador Mining and Exploration Co., 71
Land Settlements, 96-98
Lansbury, George, 115
Lapland, 100
Lebanese, 17
Legislative Council, 21-22, 27, 47
Lever Bros., 76-78
Lewis Hills, 9, 70
Lewisporte, 41
Liberals, 22, 110, 144-146
Library Service, 127
Liquor Control, 117
Liviers, 15, 101, 140
Lobster Fishery, 56
Lobster Controversy, 23
Local Government, 38-47
Local Government Department, 40, 43, 46-47
Long Range, 9, 59-60, 92
Louisiana, 61, 102
Lourdes, 18, 128

Macdonald, Sir Gordon, 7, 28, 35, 110
Magistrates, 20, 37-38, 43, 46
Marconi, 89
Margarine, 34, 76-77
Maritime Provinces, 34, 54, 57, 81-88, 105-108, 147-148
Meals, 117-118
Merchandizing, 74
Memorial University College, 37, 120-127, 138
Methodists, 15-16, 32, 120
Micmacs, 11, 17
Miners' Union, 109
Miquelon, 12-13
Monroe's Fishery Products, 52
Moravians, 8, 15-17, 140-142
Mount Pearl, 96, 100

Nain, 90
National Park, 63
Natural Resources, Department, 35, 48, 52, 94-96
New England, 13, 53
New York, 56, 87

Newfoundland Federation of
   Labour, 109
   Industrial Development
     Board, 77
   Hotel, 35, 118
   Labour Party, 110
   Railway, 70, 81
   Teachers' Association, 109
Nomenclature Commission, 18
Nonconformists, 15
Nonia, 99, 134
Northcliffe, Lord, 60
Northwest River, 15, 101, 141
Notre Dame Bay, 68, 80
Nova Scotia, 11, 56, 68-73,
   105, 124, 140-148
Nutrition, 132-134

Old Age Pensions, 137
Ontario, 17, 148
Opposition, 22
Orphans' Pension, 137

Paper Makers' Union, 109
Paper Mills, 59-62
Pattison, Sqr. Ldr., 7, 86
Pensions, 137-138
Petty Nord, 14, 53
Place Names, 17-19
Placentia, 12, 37, 88, 152
Police, 48
Poole, 12
Post Office, 35, 88-89
Port-au-Port, 70, 71, 99, 128
Port-aux-Basques, 53, 61, 80,
   83, 103, 113
Port Hope Simpson, 66, 141
Port Union, 24
Portugal, 11, 57
Progressive Conservatives, 110,
   145-146
Protestants, 16
Provincial Affairs, Ministry, 48
Public Health and Welfare,
   Department, 36, 132-138
Public Works, Department, 48
Public Utilities and Supply,
   Department, 36, 40-43

Quebec, 57, 71, 139-143

Radio, 34, 89-91
Railways, 25, 34, 80-82
Rangers, 35, 48, 113, 142
Referenda, 30-33, 145
Reid Interests, 60, 72, 80
Reindeer, 100-101
Relief, 136-137
Religious organization, 15-17
Representative Government, 21
Responsible Government, 22-41,
   82, 144
Roads, 39-41, 82-85, 113
Road Boards, 39-41
Robinsons, 18, 84, 92, 97-102

Salmon Fishery, 50-51, 112,
Salmonier, 60, 63
Salt, 56-57
Salt Cod Fish Trade, 49-55, 139-
   140
Salvation Army, 16-17, 121, 126
Saw Mills, 59, 62-63
St. Anthony, 37, 53
St. Georges, 7, 37, 83-84, 92,
   97-98, 102, 152
St. John's, 10, 16-17, 21-45, 53,
   57-63, 70-76, 80-128, 135, 151
St. John's Housing Corporation,
   38, 45, 128-130
St. John's Town Council, 38,
   45
St. Lawrence, 10, 23, 53, 70
St. Pierre, 12, 13
School Boards, 120
Scott, Magistrate, 7
Scottish, 11, 15, 17
Sealing, 50, 56
Secondary Education, 122
Settlement (of Newfoundland)
   11-14
   (Labrador), 15
Shack Towns, 39, 130-131
Shipbuilding, 77-78
Shop and Office Workers'
   Union, 109
Smallwood, J. R., 31, 47, 110,
   144-146, 149
Somerset, 11, 17
Spain, 11

Springdale, 37
Steamship Services, 82, 85
Stephenville, 83-84
Supply, Department, 79, 106
Syrians, 11, 17

Teachers, 48, 125
Telephones, 89
Terms of Union, 33-34, 57, 137
Tobacco, 76
Tompkins, 18
Torbay, 87-88
Tourist Development Board, 112
Trade Unions, 109-110
Trans-Canada Air Lines, 87-88
Trepassey, 12
T.B., 132-137
Twillingate, 13, 37, 151

United Church, 15-17, 33, 120-126

U.S.A., 13, 16, 22, 31, 36, 56-71, 93, 103, 111, 118, 124, 135-148
Veterans' Affairs, 138

Wabana, 19, 68
Wages, 108
Walsh, 144
Water St. Merchants, 21-32, 106
Welfare, Department, 48
West Country, 11-17, 20-21, 74
West Indies, 23, 57
Whaling, 50, 56
Whiteway, 26
White Bay, 61, 151
Windsor, 40, 45
Winter Storage, 102-103
Workers' Educational Association, 127
Workmen's Compensation Act, 110

This book may be kept

FOURTEEN DAYS

A fine will be charged for each day the book
is kept over time.